THE STRUCTURE OF DESIRE

W.F. LANTRY

FIRST EDITION

Little Red Tree Publishing, LLC,
635 Ocean Avenue, New London, CT 06320

Copyright © 2012 W.F. Lantry

All rights are reserved under International and Pan-American Copyright Conventions. Except for brief passages quoted in a newspaper, magazine, radio or television review, no part of this book may be reproduced in any form or by any means, electronic or mechanical, including photocopying and recording, or by any information storage and retrieval system, without permission in writing from the publisher.

Layout and Cover Design: Michael Linnard
Text in Minion Pro, Trajan Pro and Ariel.

First Edition, 2012, manufactured in USA
1 2 3 4 5 6 7 8 9 10 LSI 16 15 14 13 12

Foreword © 2012 Jean-Yves Solinga

All previous publication credits of the poems in this collection are listed at the back of this book.

Front cover painting, *Miranda - The Tempest (1916)* by John William Waterhouse, (1849-1917) English Pre-Raphaelite Painter, Victorian Romanticism. Extract appears on the back cover.

Author photograph, on page 129 and back cover, was taken by Avonlee Photography and is reproduced here by kind permission.

All paintings that appear in this book are in the public domain and attributed individually.

    Library of Congress Cataloging-in-Publication Data

Lantry, W.F.
  The structure of desire / W.F. Lantry. -- 1st ed.
    p. cm.
  Includes glossary and index.
  ISBN 978-1-935656-19-7 (pbk. : alk. paper)
  I. Title.
  PS3612.A58565S77 2012
  811'.6--dc23
                      2012018801

Little Red Tree Publishing LLC
635 Ocean Avenue,
New London Connecticut 06320
www.littleredtree.com

Contents

Foreword by Jean-Yves Solinga ... vii
Prologue with Chapter Introductions by W.F. Lantry ... xiii
    I – Courtship ... xvi
    II – Attachment ... xix
    III – Hearthsongs ... xxii
    IV – Constructing Beauty ... xxv
    V – Antecedents ... xxvii
    VI – Graceful Designs ... xxix
    VII – Echoes ... xxxiii

I – COURTSHIP ... 1

    Love Sings Us From This Life ... 2
    Meteors ... 3
    The Structure of Desire ... 4
    Listening ... 5
    Catalog ... 6
    Carmina Burana ... 7
    Chanticleer ... 8
    Shorelines ... 9
    Memory ... 10
    Magic ... 11
    Sorceress ... 12
    Visitation ... 13
    Transformation ... 14
    Green Tara ... 15
    Mirabai ... 16
    Arrival ... 17
    Exploration ... 18
    Triptych ... 19
    Dalliance ... 20

Synchronicity	21
Coloratura	22
Convocation	23
Voyage de Noces	24

II – ATTACHMENT   25

Revery	26
Renewal	27
Lotus	28
Anacostia	29
Adornments	30
Prey	31
Mayday	32
Mysteries	33
Restoration	34
Revision	35
On Learning How to Read	36
Songe	37
La Belle	38
Rasa	39
Spinning Yarns	40
Miranda	41
Landscape	42

III – HEARTHSONGS   43

Flow	44
St. Thomas	45
Reflections	46
Return	47
Le Vin du Diable	48
Victimae Paschali Laudes	49
Disorder	50
Misunderstanding	51
Wrenhouse	52
Visionary	53
Storm	54
Prayer	55
Jewelweed	56

IV – CONSTRUCTING BEAUTY — 57

Talavera — 58
Hinges — 59
Mousetrap — 60
Arts and Mysteries — 61
Passionate Virtuosity — 62
Sovereignty — 63
Prosody — 64
Censer — 65
Ritual — 66
Jouissance — 67
Constructing Beauty — 68
Chateau Miranda — 69

V – ANTECEDENTS — 71

Raven — 72
Night Pearls — 73
Mirrors — 74
Melusine — 75
Redemption — 76
Columbina — 77
Sumeria — 78
Spinning Wheel — 79
Gold — 80
Silk Road — 81

VI – GRACEFUL DESIGNS — 83

Stone Cutters — 84
Labyrinth — 85
Glass Harmonica — 86
Theological College — 87
Mendelssohn — 88
Grace — 89
Evanescence — 90
Lied du Chêne — 91
Amber — 92

    Yungas Valley   93
    Rutter's Requiem   94

VII – ECHOES   95

    Folklife Festival   96
    A Tail Full of Suns   97
    Double Vision   98
    Photograph   99
    Tatu   100
    Fisher   101
    Cloud Ladders   102
    Cymatics   103
    Resurrection Fern   104
    Compline   105
    Departure   106
    The Dark Wood   107
    Incarnant Sounds   108
    Epilogue   109
    Wind   110

Glossary   112
Index of Titles and first lines   123
Publication Credits   128
About the Author   129

FOREWORD

Men loving women is a naturally occurring phenomenon. And men have subsequently taken to writing about these women in their lives through the ages. However, there is a third ingredient that is essential—lamentably too often lacking—in any attempt to create a concrete representation of this love: A genuine and talented poetic voice with which to express it to others. Thankfully that is certainly not the case with this book. In *The Structure of Desire*, W.F. Lantry places his reader at this privileged crossroad of the poetic landscape that takes us into the sanctum sanctorum of the multi-faceted magic that results from loving a woman.

Lantry's sophisticated poetry is remarkable in its capacity to outline verbally the contours of the object of desire as he attempts to describe its central presence in his soul. As a result, the work is replete with gems that are full of lyrical sorcery as in "Revery:" …

> Her song is my restraint that gently binds
> together in secluded minuet
> our figures as if drawn across the stars.

This and other passages make us travel through a setting inhabited by the descendants of Merlin where ethereal presences are palpable.

The reader is also regaled by the author's impeccable mastery of the subtle nuances of vocabulary from the writer's cultural palette. Reading this collection is a revelation of Lantry's precise and successful insertion of lyrical imagery into a self-determined poetic structure.

What an odyssey! Even the construction of cathedrals "Stone Cutters" is the source of a lyrical reflection on the symbiotic relationship between the structure and the men building it:

> Those cutters, working stone, imagined tall
> bar traces they would never see:

The laboring humanity among these enormous stones is reminiscent of Victor Hugo's *Notre Dame de Paris*.

This is what good literature should be: densely, intelligently beautiful. It is an antidote to the "Tweeter" world. This collection is a hymn to the continued possibility of the search for using art to recreate ephemeral moments of poetic alchemy. This is the case in "Mélusine:" …

> Her breasts exposed, light handed, out of time,
> bathing in wooden vessels as she sings
> in distant languages I've never heard, …
>
> where I, by chance, see polished shells adorn
> her breasts, white as the pages of a book
> I long to read after our daylight fades
> quickly, before the moon begins its climb.

Lovers of good poetry will find in Lantry a master craftsman of what can make the genre so powerful: At such times as when this world obeys its own internal physical logic. A world to which readers have traditionally escaped to read verses such as this where, as in Plato's cave, we are indirectly shown the emotional reality in the writer's heart. In "Compline:" …

> In ringing midnight, bells are not consumed
> but the lamps must be refilled, candles replaced
> How is it, then, when burning with the same
> intensity, in this transforming flare,
> that we are undiminished?

How immediate this image of the eternity of the sound of the bells relating to the eternity of his love!

❖   ❖   ❖   ❖   ❖

This collection should be read as an exemplar of how the power of an authentic poetic voice can adapt to various poetic forms. Lantry wrote the following about his poetry: "One of the questions people often ask concerns form. After all, the poems don't look or sound like the poems they're used to. They're not in *vers libre*, nor are they in a form anyone has seen before." In this collection, his reader will have models of the pre-eminence of inspiration and talent. Lantry had his formal curriculum well in hand and his technical tools sharpened but nothing could replace the immediacy of the authenticity of finding his ultimate Muse: under whatever name she appears in the text. She is the *idée fixe* that powers his drive to capture her presence: Such as the de-incarnate wind or the fleeting spark of a lover's glance. Moments such as these permeate the best poems of this collection. The following passage from "Wind" is breathtakingly beautiful simply by what is not said explicitly but rather implied. And like the lyrics by Gilbert Bécaud in *Mes mains*, it is often by filling-in spatial voids in their souls that poets find their voices on the page. These lyrics by Bécaud came vividly to my mind when I read some of these poems. I therefore will give both the French original and my English translation: *"Mes mains dessinent dans le soir la forme d'un espoir qui ressemble à ton corps…{My hands draw in the night the shape of hope in the shape of your body…}."* I find echoes of the former in "Wind:"

> …The resonance I've learned
> Is not the wind around us. If I could
> I'd let the harmonies I labor go
> And simply draw your figure in the air
> Between us, as if form and words were one.

Great loves and talent have always found echoes and correspondences of each other in other art forms and other artists. This book is an excellent example of this landscape.

Jean-Yves Solinga
Gales Ferry, CT 2012

Acknowledgements

A Few Words of Gratitude

No-one works alone. Writing seems a solitary occupation, but it only looks that way. When I sit staring at the blank screen, I have a thousand companions, each of them looking over my shoulder, encouraging me, telling me to change direction, pushing me forward. I offer these pages to them, as a gift of thanks, a small token for all they've done.

When I was young and sure of myself as only the young can be, Miriam Niethus persuaded me to read the Gita and Lao-tzu. She, and they, showed me I was on the wrong path. Even then, I had no sense of direction. Carolyn Forché cured me of that. Through her, I saw a completely different world, one I hadn't known existed. But I didn't live in it until Jacqueline Ollier plucked me out and placed me in another context. "It will change your life," she said. She was right. So was Galway Kinnell, who persuaded her, on the strength of a few poems, she was doing the right thing.

Even though I was still completely lost, Derek Walcott told me to keep going. He easily cut through some of the brambles blocking my path, and told me to ignore the rest. It was good advice. Don Barthelme guided me into a different kind of forest, filled with wondrous trees and odd statues, and helped me feel at home there. James Robison told me to sit down and get to work. Which I've been doing, even though I feel like I'm still a beginner.

And then there are the editors who believed in the work even when nobody knew my name, and printed it. June First, 2009: thanks to Kate Bernadette Benedict, Mary Ann Sullivan, and Charles Musser, twelve poems appeared that first day. It felt like I went from zero to sixty overnight, all thanks to them. I still remember that moment fondly. There have been so many wonderful editors since then: Tammy Ho Lai-Ming at *Asian Cha*. Don Zirilli at *Now Culture*. Elizabeth Savage at *Kestrel*. Meg Pokrass at *BLIP,* Annabelle Moseley at *String Poet*, Katy

Evans Bush at *Horizon Review*, Gloria Mindock at *Istanbul Literary Review*, Sarah Busse at *Verse Wisconsin*, Lacey Dunham, Joani Reese and Bill Yarrow at *THIS*. Nic Sebastian published the first interview with Kate. Meg Tuite at *Connotation Press* gave us early encouragement, as did Susan Tepper, Ed Byrne, and Amy Burns. The list could go on and on, but I especially appreciate the editors in far flung corners of the world: Eva Lindberg in Israel, Serene Taleb-Agha in Syria, Darren Carlaw in England, James Penha in Indonesia, Rati Saxena in India, Melvin Sterne in Bosnia, A'zam Obidov in Uzbekistan. One of the great joys of publishing is building relationships with interesting people around the globe.

Ned Balbo championed *The Language of Birds*, even though I'd never had a chapbook. And one day, we got an email from Michael Linnard offering to publish this collection, and beginning a long and fruitful relationship. Thank you, Michael.

Not all of the help has been literary. Marquez tells a story about his landlord who let his rent slide month after month as he worked on his first book. When the book was published, the landlord pounded on his door, saying "Please tell me I had some part in this!" Along those lines, I thank my father, Frank Lantry, a design engineer, who patiently explained over the course of years the mechanics of things, how to take them apart and put them back together, how to fix things right the first time, so they don't fall apart two miles down the road. And he taught me to not let concerns get in the way: One day, I was trying to reroute a gasline into my kitchen so I could install a new range. I stood there in the basement, staring at a run of one-inch black pipe. "Just take your Sawzall and cut through it," he said. "Won't it blow up?" "Trust me," he said. I did, and do. Virginia, his wife, my mother, is a painter, musician, and poet. And a nurse, who cared for the sick, the dying, who knows and has lived the ethics of care. I still think of my work as a combination of the best of those two sets of talents: someone who designs things, knows how they work, knows how to fix them, not worried about getting his hands dirty, and someone who creates other kinds of things, carefully, with practiced love.

These poems, this book, would not exist without Kate, their subject, their inspiration, their driving force. She waves her hands in the air, murmurs a few phrases, and gives me the energy to keep going. Finally, there's the Muse, the only one, the true one. Whenever things get difficult, I take her chaplet in my hand and ask for her help. This book is the first step in keeping my promise to her.

PROLOGUE

Marie Spartali Stillman (1844-1927). *Love's Messenger,* 1885.

Miranda:– A miraculous being, whose existence could be neither imagined nor predicted, who insists she's "just a mortal woman." A protean changeling, whose transformations, if revealed, would mystify the most jaded skeptic. The center of a whirlwind. A coloratura soprano. Also, by the grace of providence, my wife.

All the attributes of Miranda are measured in circular forms. Her waist is a meridian, her bracelet an orbit of light. In the rushed luminosity of dawn, in the declining radiance of an autumn evening, when the voices of birds are falling around us, and the owls begin moving in silence between the unclothed branches, the echoes of her singing voice move out in infinite circles. A ring constrains even her finger.

And the liquid sequences of her notes are like the fluid records of a stone skipped dexterously across a pond. The closest circle widens as the stone moves off to make another, another, all the way to the opposite bank, where it settles into silence. We can watch the circles widening, note the harmony of their continuous pattern, the straight line their centers describe, but they are always rings overlapping rings, each a small vortex of sound, a corona of notes both performed and heard. Through her breath, we pass into breathlessness, aroused and composed by her voice. When the tempo slows, when the voice moves up her scale as the dawn light moves across our earth, or as the stars move in circles through the darkening air, we long to be one of those night birds, with their secret wings, climbing along on the waves of her sound, disappearing into what has always been.

The sensuous joy of our listening, the miracle we newly sense of simply being able to hear such delight, reminds us there was a time when we knew only silence, and makes us regret that time will come again. Its beauty teaches the rapture of a particular moment, makes us desire to dwell within her space now, and in the next moment, and the next, each note a bound moment of the eternal, caught within her lips and shaped to the forms of our elations.

Driven beyond accomplishment or artistry, the trained expertise and the physics of resonate air, part of us still measures the singular rhythm, the practiced pitch of exactness, the way the tone moves from one place to the next, the way a hummingbird's wings beat in precise orbits, each feather moved by particular muscles, all of them working as one.

We have all heard *Panis Angelicus,* how many times, and *Pie Jesu*, and yet in her voice it becomes new, as if it were composed in that moment, from eternal lips to hers, infinite now in our present, and in memory imprinted as if by wood block, or engraving, as if a lithograph could bear its lines unchanging. Her voice is the sharpened burin, and we the copper plate. And if the paper is pressed against us, how could we resist replicating her form, or remaking the mark it has left in our flesh?

I have heard the learned men standing outside the Basilica, on the steps near those statues, discussing her phrasing, analyzing the pulsing undulations of her song, unable to capture in eloquent syntax even the tenth part of enduring emotion she calls with such ease to the air. Better to remember the weeping of women in the pews, my own weeping as I listened, the joy and anguish of feeling her openness, her presence among us, there on the raised dais, her arms spread wide to gather us into the flames she inhabits, and which burn within her untended.

Only surrounded by mosaic walls is she fully herself, only when her voice lingers around the marble columns lit by rose windows, her face glowing in the tinted light, the wind singing through her in windless space, does she become the one voice, her singular inflections lifting us above the incense of mourning, as if we were particles of smoke, roiled on the currents of sound moving through her, the light down of doves floating near transept arches.

And yet, we hear her words written within us. Whatever song she sings, the terms of the Lacrymosa, our sadness caught within them, like the sadness of all who have suffered. There is no comfort, but there is no despair, our sorrows made crystalline, constant but faceted, as if her voice could cleft their rough edges, and preserve beauty within loss.

So we move on, always caught in that moment, as the next song begins, unable to remember what came before, or what would follow, we live inside her and she in us, the first stanza, the following refrain. Unable to believe there could be a next moment, longing that each be the one, and endure, and yet longing to hear the grace of transition, for part of the joy is in harmony, the stone skipping, the circles merging on the water's surface, a mirror of all we've become, and everything we desire to be.

For the laid out body once had such desires, before the incense was lit, before the elegant wood was cut, and planed down by hand, before it was sanded and finished, and rough hands polished its flanks. Those feet, so still now, once ran towards a consuming passion, the lips, silent now as a stone beneath water, once spoke of a beauty like hers. And the corpse, dressed in such clothes as it wore on the brightest occasions, now is anointed with small waterdrops, and the same drops are flung into the pews, to remind us. And she goes on singing like the endless sea, or like a woman walking beside it, the spaced breakers her background chant.

Perhaps because she knows the breakers will continue? How else could she go on? Now the doors open, as her voice rises. Now the people stand, invited by her lifting arms, now they turn and watch the procession go past. The steps of the bearers match her slow rhythm. They move through the doors, and into sunlight.

But I am standing in the darkest corner, still listening. All I possess are the shadows. She gathers up the sheets of her music, and walks towards me in silence.

❖ ❖ ❖ ❖ ❖

Chapter Introductions

I. Courtship

Miranda sings. I'm constantly asking myself why I do things, but Miranda simply steps forward, sure of her purpose. My love songs have their own designs, their own histories, but hers are public, communal, reaching deep back into time, across the centuries. She sings at wedding ceremonies, her voice helping unite couples as they begin their journeys, celebrating their love with hymns. And Miranda sings at the end of their journey. When grief renders everyone else speechless, she knows the words, their order and pitch. You can hear her voice when the rest are silent. And if you listen closely, you can hear the women who preceded her, on down through the generations. History is alive within her, even while she is most fully alive within the present moment.

In certain moments, I understand her mysteries, or at least some of them. But there are mysteries everywhere, eternal things we sometimes forget to notice, or haven't yet dreampt, even if others have pointed us towards them: the sudden flash of a meteor against the night sky, the way a fire draws our gaze, and holds it, the patternless patterns of the movement of water, resonant and ephemeral at once. All these things are mirrors of each other, and of us. And if we listen closely enough, they can become part of our voice.

I knew a woman on the Côte d'Azur who loved intimate things, treasured small objects as tokens, performed whispered rituals over them. She asked me to give her some small object, anything I'd held, as if those whispers could make my heart hers. Miranda doesn't need any of those things. Oh, she keeps objects around her, small shells and candles, images of peacock feathers, accouterments and adornments. When a ray of light touches the curling smoke of incense, she is violet and indigo. She doesn't take my breath away, her presence helps me breathe.

Our very breath is the source of creation. We know this deeply, we even talk about inspiration. We all hesitate to call ourselves artists, and yet we must, if we're going to speak of the process of art. For myself, when I sit down, I become aware of a cacophony: all the voices I've ever heard, all the lines I've read and things I've seen. Slowly, one by one, I quiet each, disremember, empty my gaze. It's only when I reach silence that I can truly listen, and even then the voice is delicate, barely heard, a whisper, a song.

But one can't simply sing silence, or reproduce an endless harmonic murmur. The poems must be filled with the things of this world. Real things, the objects and tokens around us, our true landscape. Miranda brought new elements into my landscape, changed the territory I inhabit, transformed even the sounds that came to my ears. But all those are only metaphors for something deeper, something even a poet can only articulate in certain unconscious moments, an unimagined metamorphosis of being. Holding her in my arms, it occurs to me there may be more to this earth than I had known. It seems impossible, I know. I'm as skeptical as you are. And yet...

My first hint of all this came when we went to concerts together. I had heard the same music before, but now I heard it in a different way. Not through her ears, exactly, but inhabiting the space near her, I heard a deeper music, or felt as if the music were becoming me, through her. It seems beyond explanation, but how can you explain songs whose words were written seven centuries ago, and seem to prefigure her, which describe her as if she were standing in front of the poet even then? How could she, motionless, pull me out of the swirling chaos of being and place me at the still center, so I could finally see all the motion around me?

For there are moments like that, when time seems to stop. Music is sequential, one note coming after another in time, but in rare moments time changes, becoming both movement and stillness. Her favorite song is Biebl's "Ave Maria," sung in chorus without instruments: just the voices in harmony. The words aren't complicated, you already know them by heart. She told me about it, I didn't believe her. We went to hear it performed. She interlaced her fingers with mine as the song began. Reader, I wept as I listened. I'm not ashamed to admit it. Sometimes we weep with joy when surrounded by beauty.

How could I know the world contained such things? Not long before I met her, I'd traveled by train through the countryside of her youth. I'd looked out the window and seen an attractive summer landscape, the rounded green forms of trees, scattered houses painted white where the forest gave way to fields and marshes close by an Eastern sea. I looked out through the train's windows, remembering all the other landscapes I'd known. I had no idea, then, that the emotions I felt watching the scene prefigured the emotions I'd feel when she arrived.

Miranda is blessed with an indefinite memory, as if all time existed at once, a constant continuous being. For myself, I remember everything: the way the trees looked, which way the wind moved, the position of the sun, the exact time on the digital clockface when I looked over at her and knew my life had changed. Will you believe me if I say the earth came alive for me at that moment? Or that everything I'd known before was simply prologue, the distant curve of another life, the scattered remnants of experience I'd held as if they had meaning? I let them go. At last, my hands were empty.

I couldn't explain it. I kept telling myself she was magic, or there was magic within her. I tried to tell others. No-one believed me, perhaps because even the word was wrong. I'd known magic before, and this was something else. Something far deeper, limitless and vast, like a current in water we can't quite perceive, which carries us along. We can't see it, can't speak of it, we can only define it in terms of what it's not. And yet it's everything, surrounding us, the very spirit of our being.

By this point, I know what you're thinking. She sounds like a witch. You're probably looking around for her familiars. Let me put your mind at ease: she isn't fond of cats. Yes, I notice birds in her presence, but maybe they're always there, and I just don't notice. When I asked her flat out, because one needs to ask directly, she denied it. "I'm just a mortal girl," she said. Perhaps. But who says that kind of thing?

I'm a gardener. The first time she came to visit, she only wanted to see the garden: the ponds, nymphea blooming like jewels set in water, the lotus, vines, the bamboo grove. I knew cultivation is careful work, providing the right conditions for each plant to thrive. Blossoms are not chance or accident, they are indications we've done the work well. Taken together, they became a garden, and suddenly that garden had become her setting. Later, inside, I could hear the voices of doves through the open window as she walked towards me. I remember circles: a small bowl of water, a blue or red cloth. The light itself seemed to change.

I'm told Mirabai had a similar effect, centuries ago, on a distant continent. They still sing of her there, the beauty of her voice, her delicate passion, in songs filled with wind and flame and rushing wings, whose presence makes everything seem one. That's exactly how I felt whenever I knew she'd arrive soon, coming to me in the morning or at dusk, as if arriving from another shore. I keep trying, over and over, to explain that moment. But maybe there are some things we can't speak of, some things best left to song. I even tried speaking about it to her. Over and over. She simply said what she always does: "I'm just a mortal girl." There was something about the way she said it that convinced me. Reader, I married her.

❖ ❖ ❖ ❖ ❖

II. Attachment

Remember, now, those medieval studies of perspective you've seen, stretching all the way into the Renaissance. Triangles inside of circles, rectangles, disappearing lines, all somehow harmonized together. I've looked at them for years, trying to imagine their solution. Have you ever considered them, and wished for some sign, some hint of meaning? I promise you, Miranda is the key. To watch her simply walking is to understand the fascination of those old masters, to see her turn and bend is to share their vision, and when I hear her voice, I understand even their most intricate solutions.

The mystical saints in every religion speak of the unity of all being, of how, if we could only see, everything is harmonized. I never believed any of them, since I'm no saint, but since I've known Miranda I've begun to wonder. Not that suddenly everything is unified, that all is interconnected, merging together in a single form. It's far stranger than all of those: she can become anything, and everything, at once or in sequence. It makes me wonder if the tale of Proteus is true: someone can change, over and over, and my role is simply to hold her, to keep her grounded enough so she feels completely free to transform into whatever she imagines.

Is she a lotus bud, held above the water by my arms, opening into the sunlight? Yes. And the small sparrow singing from the branch above the pond, the flowers opening in dappled shade, the pattern of geese in the wind above us, all in sequence, all at once. Therefore,

I try to catch the moments as they pass, never to be recovered: the way her face looked in the cold autumn wind, beautiful as only gemstones can be, as she sat on a chiseled granite bench, the cherry boughs her setting.

And all this opened my eyes to another world, so different I sometimes question my own grasp of reality. I'm a woodworker after all, and a gardener. I've had to learn how to follow the wood grain with the sharpened edge of a shoulder plane, how to care for tender seedlings if they're to become trees. There's no magic involved, nothing but craft, skill, and knowledge. And yet, the forest seems alive since I met Miranda, the woods behind our home seem filled with miraculous creatures I can name, and just across the river I can see figures dancing in the sunlit meadows by the treeline.

But the miracles I see there are nothing compared to the miracles I experience within our curtained room. Nothing should seem mysterious there, I hung those curtain rods myself. I made the bedframe in my shop, I know exactly how the wood is joined, how the canopy is held aloft, even the bedside bowls were turned on my lathe. Still, even though each is a fabricated object to me, in her presence they become her adornments, everything around her somehow changed. My art is her artifice, my skills transformed by her into unimagined harmonies.

But it's never as gentle as you imagine. In ancient Greece, they told stories of women who would run through the wild lands, naked, chasing their prey. And when they caught whatever they were hunting, deer or rabbit or bird, they would tear it apart, and feast on its flesh, then run off, stained in blood, pursuing new quarry. I always thought that was just a legend. Now I know it's real. Sometimes, as I hold her, she transforms into one of them, or into a leopard, or an eagle. When she first bit into my flesh, I thought to myself: "Let her feed, if she needs to. I have strength enough." I thought of Prometheus, how the eagle consumed him, how his flesh grew back the next day. And so I held her, turned my neck, and offered her my shoulder.

I'm still uncertain about the nature of love. We all talk about it, believe we know something of it, as if we understood all its secrets. But we're still surprised when we encounter some of its forms. Even the act itself is a mystery. We talk about 'making love,' in the French sense of 'faire l'amour.' But do we literally mean it? Can we fabricate it, as a made thing, craft it, literally call it into being? I will tell you now a secret honest truth: at certain moments I can actually feel it flowing into the world through the two of us. Some people talk of prayer that way, how while they whisper they can feel grace moving through them, as if their words, or something about them at that moment, were a conduit into our world. I don't know, I've never personally experienced that. I only know what I've felt myself.

Please don't misread. I don't mean to say I understand any of this, that Miranda is a mystery revealed, a Gordian knot untied. The undefined transcendence of her being fascinates me, the consummation of her votive will as we become intertwined, as the wind envelops us. It's only a slight movement of the air, immeasurable, but so real I can feel it swirling around us. "Make the wind come," she whispers to me, but I'm not the one who causes its arrival. I'm only the one who watches, who notices, who sees her hair moving slightly when the wind arrives, who feels it lightly against my skin.

In certain moments, I believe this is all new, and unique. In others, more often now, I realize this is how things have always been. Miranda simply restores things to their true nature, or reveals them again. Water and wind and light, and the interplay of harmonies between them. A candle, a small bowl of water, the wind I've discovered through her. And her voice, whispering the ritual only she can hear, in words I cannot repeat. I only know the accoutrements, the implements of her desire: petals and salt, incense and cloth. The necklace against her skin.

And afterwards, each night, I fall asleep, losing consciousness. I'm convinced I no longer dream. In the morning, I wonder what's happened. Can any of this be real? We have to reconstruct the world each morning as we wake back into it. I remember, in the sunlight, her song, sung in near darkness. At least some of it. I remember the way she nearly danced as she walked across the room. It all comes back to me, slowly.

I remember reading, the night before, as I always do. Ancient stories, handed down to us, before they were nearly forgotten, nearly lost, the old tales I love the most. I get absorbed into them. The only thing that breaks me free is her voice, singing. I put the book down and watch her undress. The clothes go, one by one, layer by layer, onto the rocking chair, or simply fall to the floor I refinished with my own hands. Her songs then are like those old stories, they have their origins in a different time, which she makes real, and brings to life. She breathes life into them, and into me.

And even though I no longer dream, she still does. Sometimes, in the daylight, she recounts her dreams, not knowing how often they've been brought to life. Houses or hidden rooms, lost objects, inscribed bracelets. I listen, and sometimes write them down. She asks me to explain them, but what could I tell her? Perhaps it's enough to simply get the details, as accurately as possible, and make a record of them. Finding their meaning is for wiser men than me. I am simply her witness.

I hope that's enough. More than enough, a full time occupation. I am the witness to her rose, her ice blossomed forest, the restless cobalt waves of her oceans, her lavender mirrors and evening clothes. I love all of them, every detail, and through those details, her.

Every poem ever written, every autumn turning it gold leaves and loosing them to the wind, every monument of bronze or marble, I see every form in her. Every sunset, every wind, all the incantations across the centuries, the ones I knew by heart, the ones I only thought I remembered, each is in her voice. And her voice is in them, every time I turn, in every sound I hear, I listen deeply to her.

Miranda delights in stories, and I tell her the ones I've learned. When I tell them well, I know right away. Her response is quick, complete, all-consuming. I can feel her breath, the warmth of her skin, the way women at spinning wheels could once tell by feel every detail of the thread between their fingers. The stories they told each other then were like the ones I whisper to Miranda now.

Early on, she asked me to tell a story of our future together, she asked me to write it down. She must have breathed inspiration into me, somehow I got the details right. Or maybe its something far more interesting than that. Perhaps by writing things down, we call them into life, we imagine reality, and make it real. I'm not sure. All I know is I wrote what she asked, and it has all been accurate so far.

Or is it that our lives mimic something outside of us, or that the landscape really does repeat us? As without, so within, as someone said. On the coldest of winter nights, Miranda wears a red flannel nightgown, with a white printed pattern. I look at her, and think of the redbrick of our exterior walls as the snow falls against them, and of the warmth within, enemy of snow.

❖ ❖ ❖ ❖ ❖

III. Hearthsongs

I traveled with Miranda to Chincoteague, where the small horses still live along the beach. I had to look up the foreign shorebirds, tiny white things with triangular wings in the sunlight. I was so busy watching them I didn't notice the mist coming in, and didn't notice how close the horses had come. I always do that, focusing on what's near at hand, missing the vision across the dunes. They'd seemed so far away.

We went to the Virgin Islands, they felt almost like home. I'd hoped for paradise, a lush blossoming, but the islands are nearly arid, beloved of iguanas, sea snakes and sharks. From the cliffside I could see them prowling the cove: we stayed in shallow waters, walking the tidepools, the exposed reef at low tide. Miranda cut her foot on an urchin, I had to carry her back to shore, and dress her wound.

Back home, our son didn't mean to break the mirror in his room. He didn't actually do it. He was just standing there when it happened to fall. He didn't touch it. There were mirrored fragments everywhere, each reflecting a different scene, at sharp edged angles: birds outside the window, trees. I gathered them up thinking of other mirrors, a box I'd seen once, lined with silvered glass, Miranda in her looking glass, brushing her hair. I wish I could recapture every image of her, save them close to me before they disappear.

It's these daily scenes that should be all of our art. Two deer grazing near the roadside as we drive by. Even young James wants to hold that image in his mind, to return to the same place, find the same deer, standing exactly there. He loves his life, and hopes to recreate each moment. He wants me to feel what he feels when he looks at them; he wants me to share his joy.

But there's more to it, the greater part of art is the process itself. Poets should be makers of things, even if others consider what's made mundane. Yes, they have to know the true names of things, have to be able to see, and sing, but most of all they have to know how things are made. How is wood planed, how is stone set, how are bridges built, how does one turn grapes into wine? Poets should have pragmatic answers for these questions.

And for other questions as well. I took James to church on Easter. I expected him to revel in the scene, the ritual, the songs. He was so full of life and energy he couldn't sit. He fairly burst through the doors to the outside, running through the light and the air, climbing a tree in his good clothes, watching the scene. He asked what was happening, and I didn't have the words to say in a way he could understand. So he supplied his own.

He has little patience for what another poet called 'the blessed rage for order.' Because he sees me using garden tools, he breaks into the shed and does the same, scattering the tools all over the garden as another captures his interest. He has that kind of energy. Once, he got out some cans of paint, mixed the red and white, and painted the shed. And himself. And some of the stairs.

The same disorder seems to have infected the seasons. Two years ago, winter stayed late. This year, we had no winter. Back then, I waited as long as I could to plant the tender spring bulbs, tried to nurture them through the long wait. But everything's become unpredictable, the mockingbirds hardly know when to return now, and I find wrens nesting in my shop.

I had to provide another place for them: too much noise, too much activity. So I mounted some wood on the lathe and stared turning a new home for them. James stood across the shop, watching. He's not old enough to hold a bowl gouge or a skew chisel, but he's old enough to help sand, and he loves working on things. He loves to rework them. I think that's what happened to the wrenhouse two seasons later. He meant to improve it, and knocked it down. The best is the enemy of the good.

There's one thing I can count on in every season: the beauty of Miranda. I was first taken with her in cold weather, and believed she was a Winter. There are scenes I hold in my mind: descending a hillside in a blizzard, and finding her standing in the snow in a blue coat. Her face as she sat on a stone bench in even colder weather, the air as clear as I've ever seen, her jewel tones dazzling in the sunlight. So I was surprised when Spring arrived, and that seemed her most beautiful season. And surprised, again, when Summer arrived.

Summer also brings hurricanes. If you've ever been in one, you know the emotion: you can feel something happening out over the water. Even when you can't see it, you know what's coming, how the wind turns on itself, how the air grows light and heavy at once, how the sky will darken. I know there's nothing for it, but I always want to prepare. I worry about the trees. Miranda just celebrates the ones that survive.

Perhaps it's a matter of belief. I see rain clouds above the mountains and know the river will overflow its banks tomorrow. But she has another way of looking at the rain, the way other women saw it, centuries ago. What begins as a tiny prayer or wish gathers strength as it flows down the slope and mixes with others.

It moves through the canyons and spreads into valleys, pausing at lakes, cascading over waterfalls. I see the rain, now, through her.

Some ancients thought the gods dropped letters in the streets, each one signed. Others believed every ailment had its cure, and the gods marked the plants they'd meant as curatives, signing each one. They even called it the Doctrine of Signatures: Lungwort, Bloodroot, Wormwood, all somehow indicate what they were designed to treat. Still others held that every evil has a corresponding good, and these always appear close by. Jewelweed always thrives close to wherever poison ivy grows. One can't make oneself immune, but at least the cure is close at hand.

❖ ❖ ❖ ❖ ❖

IV. Constructing Beauty

We've come to be suspicious of discussions of Art. As well we should be: wild claims are thrown around, ungrounded opinions only experts can follow. Better, perhaps, to come at things a different way: Miranda wanted a new kitchen. I promised to build it for her. It's a work in progress. One of the main steps, once I'd built the double oven cabinet, rewired and replumbed everything, installed the sink, was to craft the counter. She'd picked out Talavera tile. We worked on it together. She knows exactly what she wants.

Before I met her, I'd mostly built things for the garden: trellises, fences, gates. I always went for the rustic look. If something lasted two years, it was good. These days, things get built for the long term. Even gate-hinges are installed more carefully. I make templates, and keep them at hand. Just in case.

Since we live on the edge of the forest, there's wildlife everywhere. Birds and snakes, deer and mice. When a bedroom mouse woke her, she insisted I act. I stood in the hardware aisle, surveying the choices. Maybe I've gone soft, but the spring traps seemed savage. I chose something else, something a little more elaborate. The timorous beast went for it the first night. We let him go, outside, in the morning.

Miranda has family in Vermont, on wooded acres. Bowl turning is a civilized task, but there's also rough work involved: chainsaws, axes. The process of changing green wood to a finished bowl seems very much like transforming lived experience into a poem. Especially since her aunt, who no longer gets to Vermont, can have an object made of that wood close at hand. For daily, pragmatic use.

Elizabeth Savage is a writer and editor who lives in West Virginia. She said she'd like to use a poem, but would I be willing to change a couple words? About that time, I was building an island in Miranda's kitchen. I rerouted the gas lines, drilling up through the ceramic floor, and had to run new power cables. If it were me, I'd just make it work. But Miranda wanted those cables restrung. "Leave them like that," she said, "and I'll always know."

Our land slopes down to the river's floodplain, where the forest begins. There's a glade a little ways in, a flat open space, a little wild. I've civilized it, mowing it twice a year, making a place to sit. One year, I waited a little too long to clear the fallen winter branches, to mow. Unknown to me, hornets took up residence there. Picture the scene, I was running at speed, tearing off my clothes (the hornets had gotten under the fabric), jumping into the river, standing there, defeated, naked. I won't tell you all the places where they stung me. Allow me some small dignity.

Hornets, wasps, yellow jackets, bees, we have everything. Giant lumbering woodbees drill into the deck, so many I had to rebuild its supports. It's one story tall, up in the air, we dine in what feels like the forest canopy. The wrens love it, there are a dozen places to nest. At different times of year, we have to keep our voices down, to avoid disturbing their brood.

In an old house, everything becomes a project, or several projects. It's easy to type, "I had to rebuild the deck supports," but it took weeks, and more tools than I'd care to list. I try to clean up the shop between each project, but even that takes a day or two. There are so many tools, so many jigs, so many relics of other projects. Picking up a scrap of wood can be like biting into a Madeleine: I recognize each, and remember how they were used.

Every project has a reason, and begins with hope. But many don't succeed, don't serve their intended use. I once made a bench for an old woman who was recovering from an illness. I thought she could sit there while she was recuperating, but before I was even finished, she took a turn for the worse. Her husband sat on it for years, remembering her. And I built a room in this house, whose purpose was lost before I was done. Fortunately, Miranda knows the rituals of reclamation.

All this may seem like a lot of work to you, and it is. But it also means that even a simple walk through the gate, across the yard, up the deck stairs, and into the kitchen, is remade, reinvented, revalued. Each step is a reminder of all we've done together, the realized embodiment of possibilities. There's something to be said for that. Especially when I finally make it into the house, and Miranda's there, smiling.

So why not see, in even fallen trees, something else. A honey locust fell in an ice storm. What else was I to do, except break out the chainsaw, turn the trunk into rounds, cut them in half and mount them on the lathe? There's something satisfying in the intricacies of the process. It only takes a few minutes, but involves a thousand small techniques, learned over years. Imagine standing in front of a chunk of wood, turning at several hundred revolutions per minute, with only a sharpened steel blade in your hands, and you'll appreciate the dilemma.

All this has taught me to appreciate the work of others, and its impermanence, even more. There's an old château in northern Europe, which was beautiful before the war. Abandoned now, the forest is taking it over. Even though the staircase has fallen in, you can still see the routed marble handrails attached to the wall, the bevels, the plaster, the well-laid flooring. All our careful work, all the hand crafted details- everything falls in the end. That's what it says at the end of The Wanderer: "so always this middle earth fails and falls." And still I take care to get the mitered angles exactly right.

❖ ❖ ❖ ❖ ❖

V. Antecedents

For years it hung in my office: a painting of a standing woman in a flowing blue gown, holding a rabbit in her hands, the full moon her backdrop. There was a legend, written in Chinese characters I couldn't read, down the right hand side, some small red stamps randomly placed long after the image was painted. One day I grew curious, but knowing neither the title nor the artist, I could only research the iconography. It didn't take long to find the story: an archer, for his service to the gods, is given the herbs of immortality. His wife steals them and has to flee, hiding first in a cave, and then flying to her only sanctuary, the moon itself.

It may be night pearls are also mythological, rough translucent blue stones giving off a subtle glow when warmed by the body. Enough light to read in a dark room, enough to see. There are obscure references in ancient literature, hints and guesses. Mostly we read of them gathered in bowls still warm from the fire. But think of a necklace made of them, the rough stones illuminating her skin, casting their shadows everywhere.

We rarely think of Aphrodite's second child. We all know Eros, god of love and maybe even lust. He had his own cult, his own temples, arrows crafted just for him. But how often do we think of his brother, Anteros, god of requited love, of enduring passion? And why are they always depicted in conflict, fighting with each other? Aphrodite stands between them, holding a pair of scales, as if to say the two must be balanced, each measured in relation to the other.

Melusine's mother was a Naiad, a water nymph, a spirit of sacred springs and rivers. When a man saw her, he fell in love and proposed marriage. She agreed, on one condition: that he never watch her bathe. After many years, the temptation became too much, he spied on her and saw her true mermaid form. She took her daughters and hid in the countryside. When Melusine became a woman, a young man saw her and proposed. She accepted, on the same condition. He couldn't resist either, and lost her in the same way. Perhaps there's a lesson there.

It's one we need to learn, one we keep forgetting and relearning, over and over. We all know how the peacock's feathers shine in the sunlight, we've all watched them turning in circles, almost as if their hundred eyes can see. But what of the grackles, smaller, indistinct birds, a drab brown in the shade? If you wait, if you watch closely, they will step into the sun, and their feathers will blaze up, indigo and violet, even in the most accidental moments, an unexpected testament of grace.

Sometimes I think there's a little of every woman in Columbina, the character of operas and comedies. She's far more complex than her authors pretend, she resists the roles they write for her. Sometimes I think she already understands the plans and devices they and her leading men have in mind. She doesn't need to hear the stage whispers, or hide behind curtains as the strategies are revealed to the audience. She already knows the script, and she's determined to rewrite it in her own way.

It's been the same for going on five thousand years, all the way back to the earliest poems we have. They were found on the clay tablets in the ruined temples of Sumeria, the whole story laid out even then. Even then, men had their schemes and designs, their craft and artifice. But it wasn't a man who first descended to the underworld, who first negotiated those hidden passageways. It was a woman, and she survived everything, bringing back the gifts we all need. The rituals honored her for centuries.

And there were other rituals, shared among women in spinning rooms, as they performed the long work of turning flax into thread. They would set their wheels in a circle, and an old woman would sit at the center, recounting all the stories she knew, tales men have never heard. These are the secrets we wonder about, the hidden truths of Melusine's heart, and of Aphrodite's mysteries. Think of what that old woman knew, imagine the tales she had to tell.

One of them may have told the origins of the very thread they spun. It's said the goddess gave flax seeds to a young woman, a country girl in tattered clothes, and whispered the secrets of cultivation in her ear. The goddess' robe was blue as the flax flowers themselves. Even now, when some of those secrets have been lost or forgotten, we still see her in blue. But the linen thread emerged a rough white, and was dyed yellow, red, or even gold, with whatever the women who spun it had on hand.

On the other side of the earth, they wove silk instead of linen. The process held just as much mystery. A few years ago, one of the most graceful women alive was practicing her dance, getting ready for a performance that would be seen around the world. She leapt from one part of the stage to another. Something went wrong, and she fell. But even if she can no longer dance, I still see her that way, the way I wish to see all of us, moving through the air, through the space of our lives: exquisite, elegant, unbounded, undefined.

❖ ❖ ❖ ❖ ❖

VI. Graceful Designs

I admire the skills of stone workers, precision matched with strength and craft, and a sense of larger work. Each hammer blow dresses the block, which must be made so it fits with the work of others. And as each stone is set, it takes its place among the others, until the whole structure rises, a collective shared design. It took a century to build a cathedral, the designer knew he would never see the result of his drawings, the masons who laid the blocks even halfway up the walls knew they'd never see the roof enclosed, the glassworkers who crafted the rose windows had no knowledge of those who, three generations before, had laid the foundations buttressing their work.

Their collective work provided a space for contemplation. Even the floor of the cathedral was inlaid with a purpose in mind. Look carefully, and you can see, in the tile design, the outlines of a labyrinth. Some of them are built with a single continuous curve, and are called unicursal. You are meant to walk slowly along it, around and around in an inward spiral toward the center, pausing, contemplating. The tile workers laid a rose design in the center, and the lines of the quadrants radiate out from there. Think of the thousands who have walked that same curving path for centuries, but remember that every experience of the space is different from all the rest.

The makers of musical instruments are like those stone cutters, those tile workers. They invent something, and craft it into being. To simply see a glass harmonica is to admire both inventiveness and skill. But there's even more there: to play it requires another kind of talent, to write music that takes advantage of its possibilities still another. You've probably never seen one because of their reputation. They were said to drive sensitive young men and women in the audience to madness. People literally swooned in their seats, overcome by the sound.

Everywhere we go, if we are sensitive enough to what's around us, we are influenced and changed by the work of others. It's enough to simply walk through the hallways of old buildings, to see the way windowframes are set, how the glass was made, the gardeners' work through those panes. There is Art in each of those tasks, no less than in the sculptures, the crafted ornaments of polished marble, the icons made by one artist and framed by another.

The music we hear in such spaces is remade by them, even as it bears its own traces of creation and its own history. Not all of its stories are uplifting. Mendelssohn's Elijah may be a testament of divine fire, but it's also a story of unspeakable savagery and blood. To hear it performed is to be witness to our worst impulses as well as our best, the entire range of human experience in a few choral movements.

Flannery O'Conner saw that whole spectrum of experience and wrote about it, the best and worst at once, often in the same person. She had a penitent's humility, but chose to surround herself with peacocks. They perched everywhere around her garden, roosted in the trees, guarded the top rails of her gates, displaying a tail full of suns to even the most accidental visitor. Their calls carried for miles. Every time I hear one, I think of her.

The poet Horace was a bit of a peacock, proud of his work, boasting he'd made monuments more lasting than bronze. Other artists have different interests. The ephemeral figures made in Polynesia are designed to crumble into dust, as a kind of reminder. The elaborate sand paintings of certain Buddhists, brilliant in their colors and intricate in their designs, exist for a few days or weeks before the multicolored sand is swept up, placed in urns, and poured into a river or a stream: anything that flows eventually to the sea.

Their ceaseless recurrence, their constant cycles of transformation and becoming, makes them somehow imperishable. The oaks and vineyards of Southern France are like that. How many other poets have written about those same oaks and vines, the eternal maquis of the surrounding hillsides? It's difficult to look at such scenes and not think of René Char, to write of them is to honor him, and all the poets before him who wrote across those landscapes.

Or to walk along the shorelines of Northern Europe, finding the amber that washes up at the edge of the sea: how can we not think of all the others who have scoured these beaches for the fossilized remnants of branches, their life-sap become stone? Or think of the hands fabricating it into bracelets and necklaces, the artifice of beauty, the wrists and breasts transformed in the golden light of their work. Those artisans had to reinvent their methods for each piece.

What stays with me is their ingenuity, the way they re-engineered solutions based on whatever they found in front of them. In the mountains of Bolivia, a man was faced with a problem: his crops only grew on the ridge, and a valley hundreds of feet deep separated them from the road. How could he get back and forth to tend them? So he strung steel cables from one ridge to the other, and hung a wheeled pulley on each cable. He almost literally flies to his daily work. He speaks sometimes, in quiet moments, of repressing a sudden impulse to simply let go.

I feel for him, I've had that same impulse. Everything is so constantly tightly strung. Certain movements of music have that effect on me. I know I should pay attention, focus on the harmony and progressions, allow it to lift me and carry me along with it. But sometimes I long for other things, perhaps driven by the music to desire something else, to leave my seat and wander outside the auditorium and into the surrounding forest. In the woodlands, we feel most at home.

VII. Echoes

Since I strive for complete openness and perfect honesty, I must confess I sometimes feel like a host guiding guests through hidden rooms and secret gardens. But the Folklife Festival is held in the open air on the Mall in Washington, always in midsummer, always in the warmest weather of the year. You can wander from one demonstration to the next: dancing jeeps, complex structures made of simple canes of bamboo, palm nut ivory turned on a lathe. The artist's words are translated.

Not far down the Mall, you'll find the Freer Gallery. It's one of the first places Miranda took me. She lured me there with the promise of Asian Art, but her secret agenda concerned Whistler's Peacock Room. The place is a miracle of green and gold, of blue and white pottery, painted screens and exotic portraits. There's an original story of contention, but the only hints of difficulty are now found in the forms of fighting birds. You wouldn't guess their meaning without a guide.

I was so overcome by it all, or by Miranda, we had to step outside for a little while. People call this the Stendhal Syndrome: you can be overwhelmed by too much beauty, start feeling dizzy, develop double vision. Stendhal literally swooned in a gallery in Florence and had to be hospitalized. There have been hundreds of cases since. That was the first time it happened to me. Now, since I'm near Miranda constantly, it's become my normal state. I can't remember living any other way.

It does take a little getting used to. The best way I have to describe it concerns angled mirrors. You likely have some of these around your home, perhaps a mirrored medicine cabinet in whose open door you can see another mirror. You can see your own face reflected back and forth between the panes, over and over, a hundred, a thousand times if you hold the mirror just right. But it's always your own image you see, and so you feel grounded. Now imagine looking into those reflections and seeing not your own, but Miranda's image, infinitely replicated across time and space as you gaze at her.

In the presence of her artifice, even a trip to the store becomes an investigation into the nature of beauty, or a reminder of the meaning of Art. Our cashier really did have an unusual tattoo on his arm: the text of a poem honoring one of his ancestors. I looked at it in wonder. Imagine the time he went through to have that done, the pain, the blood, the needle piercing his skin and diving into his flesh, again and again, a hundred times a word. People ask me why I'm so careful with every line I write, and this is my answer: we should all write as if every word were going to be written literally into flesh and blood. Imagine how much he loved that poem to have it tattooed onto his skin.

Yeats said whenever he wrote he imagined a fisherman climbing up a mountain alone at daybreak, searching for a freshwater stream, a place to cast a fly. He wanted to write just one poem for that fisherman, a poem "maybe as cold / and passionate as the dawn." But Yeats doesn't talk about the fisherman's skill, the flit of his split-cane rod, the s-curve of the line as he places the cast in the exact part of the stream, in the magic hour, while there's still shade on the water's surface but sunlight on the peaks behind him. And he doesn't discuss the way a Golden Trout rises to take the fly, the flick of the fisherman's wrist, the jeweled skin coming at last to hand.

Perhaps the whole process was foreign to him, as foreign as ancient Chinese maxims are to us. If we think about them, the arguments they made can shock us out of our complacency. Of course an egg has feathers, even if we normally don't think of an egg that way. Because we value straight-grained trees, the only ones that survive in the forest are bent and twisted. Should we treat others as we wish to be treated? A king, when he arrives, expects fanfare and gongs clanging. But if a bird flew into the King's garden and he greeted that bird with the same clanging gongs, the bird would fly away.

All this makes me wonder about the sounds around us. Listening to Miranda, I consider the form of sound. I saw a video of an experiment: a steel plate was suspended on strings, its surface scattered with grains of salt. When a violin bow was drawn across the steel edge, the metal resonated, and the salt danced into patterns. The patterns changed based on pitch, on how the bow was drawn. And people learned to read them backwards: seeing the pattern, they knew the pitch, they could even know the hand that drew the bow. Even if they changed the way the grains were scattered, the forms would replicate themselves.

The same happens in the world around us. Along the Gulf Coast, arboreal ferns stretch their runners along the limbs of trees. Every thunderstorm shakes a branch or two down. I used one of these branches to construct a natural arch over a garden gate. In dry weather, the fronds of the Resurrection Fern turned brown, shriveled and shrank. But after the next rain, they returned to what they'd always been: lush, green, alive, an example of incarnation, mysterious to all visitors.

There are examples of such mysteries all around us. Bells give off sound the way candles give off light, but bells are never consumed by their ringing. And we, in celebrating the life within us, are something like those bells: it grows stronger in us as we sing. This is one of the great mysteries of Miranda: she burns always with a gem-like flame, she lights and feeds the flame within me, by voice and hand, and yet we are never consumed, never diminished. We gain energy by giving it to each other.

Everything becomes one within the circle she casts, the light, the candle smoke, the incense, even our shadows. It often feels as if others are present, echoes of different lives, other dancers from some distant time, lit by firelight. Watching her, I can't help but think of le feu de la Saint Jean. On Saint John's Day, near the twentieth of June, people across southern Europe built fires in the central square of their town and stood around them in a ring. As the flames blazed up, they would leap through them, one by one or in pairs. Sometimes couples would jump across, hand in hand. It has a Christian name, but they've been doing it far longer than Christianity has been around: leaping through fires on the solstice eve.

And maybe there's something just as enduring in the desire to write, to create a space in which the reader can dwell for a little while, the way Miranda's voice creates a place of harmony, the way a gardener gathers the elements of the natural world together in one spot. When he's done, when he's mastered cultivation, if he succeeds, a songbird may arrive, searching for water or light, a break from the wind, a place to stand. Maybe that's what he wanted all along: a way for the songbird to draw close to him. Perhaps every poem is an invitation, or a celebration of her voice.

Perhaps every poem is an incantation, a way to give form to emotion, a literary record of her beauty. Perhaps a poem can call up something which we think is outside of us, another presence, something we only intuit. I've always loved what James Wright said: "at the touch of her hand, the air fills with delicate creatures / from the other world." But for years I didn't believe it, without Miranda I still wouldn't believe it now. It's a little like faith, we find it inexplicable, and then we meet someone with direct experience. Sometimes that leads us to our own experience. It's not rational. I can't explain it. Here's what Augustine said: "We come by love, and not by sail." There may be something there, for love, for poems, for other things...

It's hard to say. I may have been working on one thing, when I thought I was doing something else. It wouldn't be the first time. I know what I meant to do: to gather strange birds and blossoms into one place to delight her eye, to ask her to see what I see, even if only for a moment, and to have my own vision transformed through her sight. But I never imagined the wind that stirs around her, the fire that blazes about her whenever she moves, never imagined I would be changed by that fire into something else, something I never believed possible. In this, at least, Horatio agreed: there are more things in heaven and on earth than are dreamt of in our philosophies, and some of them are wondrous strange.

To find them, we have to let go of everything we've ever known. We have to make a new song, unlearn our gifts, and create something worthy of her. But is that even possible when she's constantly changing? Is it enough to simply hold her as she becomes something else, to stand in the wind that moves around her? All our devices, all our skills are consumed within the vortex of her, a cauldron where all our carefully wrought gold is melted, purged, distilled to its essence. I give her my very breath, and she breathes it back into me.

This book is dedicated to Kathleen Fitzpatrick,
with thanks and admiration.

"So may our legend last while verse endures,
And all that time my name be linked with yours."

I
COURTSHIP

"Give me yourself as matter for my song:
The songs will come back worthy of their cause..."
~ Ovid

John William Waterhouse (1849-1917).
Hylas and the Nymphs (Detail), 1896

Love Sings Us From This Life

My only gift is love: I sing light songs
to please distracted ears. The best result
is passing joy, delight, a feeling of
swift transportation to another realm
where all desire's consummate, and shared
exhausted beauty's overcome. But she

sings for another cause: at our worst times
of loss she stands, as centuries ago,
millennia, women have stood, and those
who gave us birth or love sing requiem,
so she, when none can speak, sings for us all
and more than that, sings for the lost, her voice

sweeter than any incense in still air
above us, all around, surrounding each
on separate shared journeys. After speech
and ritual what else is there but song?
She leans across the podium to touch
with only notes our loss and bear it on

across those waters, undefined, but she
through her own courage, standing in the wind
or windless space, renews ours: we go on
and sing, again, of love, after a time,
although we know we'll need her soon enough
when all our consummation's overcome.

Meteors

I have not yet discovered why the earth
spins through its hidden course. I still don't know
why, in a canoe's wake, the whirlpools
from paddles spin away. There must be rules
to govern curving patterns, track the slow
unwinding of their vortices, but these,

enfolded in the darker mysteries,
are only shadows. Here, the golden voice
of meteors reveals everything
and causes resonance. If we could sing
from that same chorus, if we could rejoice
in light moving across the sky, its gold

blazing an instant, going out, enfold
its transience within our hands, unveil
what's hidden in us, mirroring the same
ephemeral but still recurring flame,
then we could speak the luminous and frail
language of water, clearly burning, spun

within a vortex. Breaking off, a tongue
of water or of flame could then reveal
the subtle mirrors guiding us. But here
as soon as they have blazed, they disappear,
leaving shadow and silence to conceal
those patterns, never showing what they're worth.

The Structure of Desire

She did not need a skirt sewn through with coins
her perfume was enough. The dance confused
my senses, blurring motions and the notes
she whispered in the prismed candlelight,
as kohl confused the darkness of her eyes
beneath the lalique pearled chignon pin

depicting peacocks, white against dark strands
holding the light, almost as tortoise shell
divides both violet and indigo
into the figured spectrums, and the bands
of light around her movements seemed to dress
her eyes, almost as if she still applied

the polished incantations of her form
symmetrically within me, as I breathed
the incensed smoke, each element of her
considered artifice slowly became
a part of me, as oxygen becomes
our blood, our life, the vision of her hands

moving in air, the perfume on her wrists
confusing every thought, the light renewed
through crystal prisms of the chandelier
illuminating feathers of her comb
gently removed in whispers, her dark hair
falling around her eyes as music slows.

Listening

A thousand voices clamour in my head
I banish each in sequence. Some persist
until I breathe them out. Their calumny
makes peace seem unachievable today
but still I chase the silence. As they go
they leave an emptiness that's quickly filled

with any music I have lately heard
and then with lyrics I remember from
songs of my early years. They fall away
and instrumental melodies confuse
all my intentions towards their vanishings,
and then the tones of ancient instruments

come crowding in, almost as if to drink
their nourishment of me, so they can speak
and these I scatter back to wandering
with just a simple, half imagined wave,
and finally, the silence fills me: now
a tranquil emptiness can overflow

the vessel I've become. Then I can hear,
and only then, her voice. Not whispering,
almost as if a breath within me spoke
in unsubstantial syllables remade
by my own breathing into earthly sound
and set down in these lines to resonate.

Catalog

Venetian plaster, tablecloths, a long
cured string of sage, or something, I can't tell
it's wrapped in dyed provincial cloth. Sharp knives
a room all done in blue and gold, with white
above us as we dine. Vased peacock plumes:
these are the things she's brought into my life

or caused appearances. Gold peonies
a book of ivory jade, with poems carved
on each smooth page, well worn by fingers from
another continent, another time.
Etched roses done in luaun, green and red
and lilies raised up from Tibetan wood.

Or songs, Ivushka in a quiet room
lost Anachie, almost her every phrase
an unknown melody, it's not just sound
not just the way her face curves this new light
her progress crossing granite squares reminds
of what I can't remember, centuries

have passed since then. I know. Almost believe
with me. It is her gift. If you could know
her transformations, Proteus would seem
no myth, and if you felt the gathered wind
that stirs about her when she moves, then you
would come to doubt all knowledge of this earth.

Carmina Burana

We rush through all: champagne rosé, bordeaux
unchilled, unknown, she can't recall the turn
and so we come in late, and cannot meet
her friends before the songs. I can't recall
the naissance of these words, and later read
how they were lost a thousand years before.

Back then, Boethius was yet in vogue
and fortune's wheel explained our every turn.
It seems I've more to learn, or must forget–
all movements here seem new this evening.
Her lips are rose, a thousand years ago
they must have been the same, and her dark eyes

gave glances much like these. You don't believe?
Look: in the garden, now past spring, she walks
where she had passed in winter, while the snow
weighed down the vines of yet another fall.
Hard to remember now, but brutal winds
were all around us then. Who hears us now?

Fortuna, in your guises, I have turned
enough upon your ring! Grant me this wine,
and multiply these moments in her arms.
For she has spread a cloth beneath green boughs
while other music played. Let those sweet sounds
banish all memories: we are not swans!

Chanticleer

Twelve voices, singing. A constructed hymn.
What words could mirror careful harmonies?
She knows how things are made, and her delight
in listening builds revelry in me.
I'm not sure how she brought me to this place
not quite a paradise, but from the stage

soft interwoven voices fill the air,
as she and I are, careless, intertwined
her left arm curved around my right. Our glance
descends a moment to our other hands:
the fabric of my sleeve commanded gray,
the cuff white by her choice, these links are gold

since she prefers it, then my wrist, the hand
revealing veins and arteries, where blood
more warmly rushes through proximity
or so she says. There's mystery in this:
my fingers interlace with hers. Almost
our blood together flows. Her hand is small,

she doesn't know the power of her wrist.
Her cuff's decided silk, which she put on
without my asking, and her sleeve is black
which harmonizes with her eyes and hair
as entwined voices harmonize onstage
though I'm uncertain of their ancient ways.

Shorelines

I did not know her when my train traversed
the marshes of her youth, the quiet Sound
with east and west across the water, slipped
in reverence by corniched houses or
those summer gardens soon to fill with snow.
I did not know those beaches had been hers,

they seemed so foreign, not like ones I'd known
in my lost years at windandsea: the long
horizon without end, dark cliffs and swells
that ran a thousand miles undisturbed
to oleanders drinking up the spray
hibiscus limed with salt. Our shaking earth

seems even now so far from granite spurs
it's hard to see both on one continent.
But we have these in common: sand and wind
and stories half remembered pouring out
in early afternoons, or late at night
when sand and snow seem one in patterned drifts:

black as her eyes the weathered granite glimpsed
from moving windows or the western night
her lips the red of ocotillos or
of eastern august fireweed, and white
as birch or desert willow her strong legs
as she walks toward me in winter bloom.

Memory

It's easy to forget. I don't forget:
1:54. A northeast wind so strong
even bare maples danced. In jewel tones
her scarf and lips and, as I thought, her eyes
were all in harmony, and as she sang
what later I would read as goddess hymns

the world came alive. What had been still
seemed animated everywhere with light
and song and even love. I still can't say
whether the moment came from just her song
or if the wind and light confused my eyes
or if something that had been sleeping all

of my existence woke with just her glance.
I can say, since that moment, I can hear
a dancing whisper everywhere, and know
a harmony I never dared suspect.
Now at her touch the universe is filled
with that same animated wind, and I

participate, at last, in that great dance
and as we swirl through our wind swept days
around each other, I'm renewed through her
each glance or whisper, in each note I hear
the goddess singing through her and to me
a joyous song of incandescent love.

Magic

She did not ask, though others had, for some
small object of quotidian reuse
which might bear, through my handling, remnants of
some inclination one could influence-
a tie I'd worn, a pen I'd used to write
empassioned words of sudden reverie-

nor did she try to fascinate my gaze
with necklaces or silk, no jewels led
to mesmerized imaginings of light
moving in waves between us, while the smoke
of incense swirled through our evening air,
no perfume swayed intoxicated will

or turned the facets of my countenance,
she did not dance me to confusion or
touch my bare skin with ancient rites designed
to incite lust or visionary thirst
for waters that might sooth our languid flames
there were no divinations of desire,

she only sang an ancient song, and I
listened in rapturous remembrance of
the kindred phrases of a distant time
and dreaming of the scenes her voice outlined
I lost all I had known, but gained those things
I hadn't thought our world could contain.

Sorceress

In Rockville as she drank her coffee, they
came crowding into overhanging trees
above her head, their rampant voices wild
with every passion. As the rushing wind,
beating through darkened wings, flowed down to us,
they followed moving shadow when she rose.

In Galway once, along the coast, I paused
beneath a row of lindens, and looked up:
a thousand wings were tipped against the sun,
their purple blackness brighter than the stars.
I clapped my hands, and as one bird they rose,
moving towards the north along the sea.

And once, along the Sound, an old man said
Raven had stolen fire, and it burned
his wings into their darkness till he dropped
the brand among the rocks. And to this day
if you take up the stones and strike them each
together, they will give up Raven's sparks.

I cannot say. I only know: when she
arrives, the wings accompany her scarf,
their voices fill the branches and our sky.
I only know that when she sings, those beaks
grow quiet, and the flames burn in her notes,
reminding me of ancient, stolen gifts.

Visitation

The garden outside sunlit from the east,
the blossoms I had labored for consumed
within this windless luminescence of
an early autumn dawn, when she arrived
trailing behind her patterns of raw silk
in jeweled tones more inflorescent than

even those vines entwined around the frames
behind her, as she stood, pausing to light
three candles and to draw down half the shades,
and I, half sleeping still, almost believed
the hour changed to unknown instances
of radiance while incensed forms converged

around her in the polished air: her hands
a whirlwind of conjuring, and then
moving towards me, fascinated by
perhaps my sleeping air, or something else
more animate than conscious: overwhelmed
by wind rushing around us in this room

and we, the sudden center of a storm,
like vines entwined and interlaced became
a confluence of unimagined light
in which blossomed the clear jewels implied
within her voice, as singing, she became,
and I began to breath another life.

Transformation

A dove along the roofline, still unseen,
its voice the harmony of morning, soft
and nearly silent in comparison,
flies off as a door opens, and she flows
into this room, as I, awakening,
consider patterns of the surging clouds

their tumult reminiscent of long waves
breaking along an interrupted coast
and both resume within me as her song
refocuses my thoughts. I almost turn
but whispers of her footsteps hold me still
and then the pattern of her skirt, half flame

and half renewing smoke, persuades my sight
that incense, insubstantial, could renew
the patterns of those clouds, or those slow waves,
or of her hands, as conjuring the air
around us into stillness she descends
and for those moments even time remains

as motionless as patterns of her skirt
while she transforms herself, and in my arms
becomes in turn both light and breath, while I
become within her arms what she could see
before the door had opened, and that dove
still called along the roofline secretly.

Green Tara

She casts a circle somewhere in this room
I don't know how, or where its limits are.
A bowl of unknown blossoms, small blue cloth
incense and dragons, clouds, a distant sea.
Wishing I had rose petals, sandalwood,
utpalas even, I begin bereft.

For languor, of her beauty I've no words.
I could describe the waves of auburn hair
or how the open window lets small winds
caress her shoulder gently, how these birds
sing now from outside into us, or how
blue cloth can cleanse… be still, let quietude

be all, and move, or motionless receive
her gift, and know, for this first time, how wind
can enter us, and be the distant sea,
her fish, her bread, allow her to consume
even this flesh. Return, and answer all.
Now from beneath, as prism, divide light

or unify: these blossoms and the waves,
auburn and rose together, lotus, birds,
until she has what I had never known
as she, communing, grants me all, or fills
this air with unknown harmonies. Now live
as if we've crossed a sea to know this calm.

Mirabai

Her form is my enchantment, wrapped in lace
and swirling as I watch, her arms half raised
near dancing rhythm as she idly sings
the subtle hymns my words revise in her
descanting once again in ecstasy
the sharp renewal of an ancient psalm

but if her form's delimited by sight
perhaps my dazzled eyes have misconceived
the borders of her presence as she flows
along the margins of her harmonies
articulated here for my delight
but leaping to another realm, as wind

leaps from one treetop to the next, or birds
are carried on the gusts from limb to limb
or as one flame encircles weaving boughs
and soon ascends to the next spiral, sparks
falling away, as her lace falls, and she
gathers my now articulated form

into her arms as silhouette of song
an interlace of indetermined shapes
whose boundaries now are lost to rampant bliss
as flames or wind are interwoven like
voices of birds, or fingers of our hands
along each other's limbs as this light falls.

Arrival

Barely recalling patterns roseate
or sanguine leaves describe in falling, I
conjecture through this sunset how her form
conveys itself along branched waterways
and how her footsteps emulate those waves
holding the fading light along their crests

and as expectant contemplation leads
to misconceptions of carved ornaments
seeming to move in rhythm to her step
so I interpret leaves, whose falling sends
in undisclosed configurations here
as sentences veined into ornament.

Now, just as darkness overtakes our earth
and as I bring the rushlights out to guide
her passage from the other shore across
the lacquered bridge I've arched across the stream
I hear the wind recalling her, whose path
is guided by the breath we nearly share

and turning inside, light the incense she
anticipates as subtle recompense
for each step of her journey, and her cloak
scarlet, thread veined in branching gold, descends
like leaves down to the patterned barewood floor
as rose petals cascade into my bed.

Exploration

What is this wind encircling us that binds
our limbs together in this candlelight
undraped by any cloth? Dancing between
the two of us entwined, glissading down
the contours of our oiled skin, it seeks
our centers as if ardor renewed flame.

Perhaps we reimagine every breath
moving around us, bending candlelight
past golden threads discarded in the wake
of ecstasy. Perhaps our motions build
until the warmth creates a current, felt
as intuition on receptive skin?

But there's no window opening between
her form and mine, nor can senses discern
in other moments random whirlwinds,
and nothing in the intervening breath
between entanglements of roses builds
within me incandescent wakening.

My best guess leaves me silent. Are there arms
around us? Is this breath their witness, or
do bridges, hidden before candlelight
emerge in revelations of our dance
allowing unimagined passages
into this landscape of our ecstasy?

Triptych

Drawn lights. The blinds descending. No disguise
hides anything. Soundscapes engage the room
whose alternating patterns craft our frame:
my supplications answered, in her name.
Now, as laced shades are covered, light perfume
eclipses what the daylight blossomed, ground

and air, combined with water, to surround
our limbs: fresh vines, new woven, an array
of tips and trellises. We fabricate
with each renewal, figures, recreate
her breath under whose ministrations sway
both reed and branch. All shadows disappear.

Shift focus. Change the camera angle. Sheer
textures grow insubstantial. What we hold
is shared with yet another. Through the air
descending now between us, as in prayer,
the space around us fills, her hands enfold
our motions. Now, as we become, so she

renews herself. Our patterned ecstasy,
unseen by any mirror, builds, cascades
as if the wind, through sudden waterfalls
dancing between the stream and rock, recalls
our earliest constructions. Now what fades
remains as afterimage in our eyes.

Dalliance

The red cloth in a basin, lavender
candles already burning, and the light
obscured by curtains, I prepare the scene
for her arrival, calculating where
the unmixed wine may best be placed and how
the covers turned back carelessly convey

deliberated messages. If once
I think of some detail, why not try
constructing every artifice for her
delight or rapt enjoyment in my arms?
Why not pursue each stratagem combined
or separately as subterfuge? Incense

alone or mixed with candlesmoke may guide
her thoughts toward some end, or may induce
some reminiscence of a watercourse
by which she once relaxed in sunlight as
the mountain breeze fingered her autumn clothes
as she half slept distracted by the boughs

waving above her. Let my hands be wind
beneath the silken rhapsodies she bears
by her own calculation, as the light
throws shadows on those curtains, patterned by
our movements through the afternoon, until
incense and candles conduit our sleep.

Synchronicity

Mistrust my words, take all in wariness
or outright disbelief. I vacillate
myself, and I was there. One evening
disquietude surrounded me. Alone
I looked into the darkness gathering
outside my windowframes. Her voice remained

within me, resonant, although she'd flown
to distances I could not comprehend
since I had never wandered that same path
so could not follow. Yet I felt her hands
caressing me. I know. Incredulous
against my own experience, I turned

encompassed by her presence, redefined,
unbound even by flesh, untethered from
even her body's limitations, she
was present, definite, enveloping
my arms in interwoven movements as
I waited, motionless. Her veiled curves

were undulations in the candlelight,
those flames that shimmered as she, silent, breathed
or sang within me, near beatitude.
The gathered ecstasy her voice awoke
rushed out, to her. I know. This cannot be.
Mistrust, refute, or disbelieve. But know.

Coloratura

I cannot step outside myself for you
nor any else: I am my prisoner
and wander aimlessly through these my woods.
My mind is empty, burning, full of wind
unfueled by the motions of the earth
or gravitated currents of the stream,

and yet, when watching how you move, at ease
around a room, or stride across a square
the track your heels make on marble, flame
or jeweled red your scarf or shawl, your song
unweaving strands of swirling light, you flow
into these woods, imagined as your limbs

their bark as smooth as birches in the rain
choirs of nightingales near morning or
of mockingbirds at noon, your voice enshrined
in noted measures, contemplations of
the interlace of patterned beauty with
forests, half wild, awakening at dawn

as I awoke this morning watching you
I felt your motions loosening what held
me captive, felt the earth in bloom, and knew
at last the meadows of my wanderings,
and these few words came flowing to my mind
as I rushed out into the jeweled wind.

Convocation

Strange mysteries of incense and of smoke
are swirling through me as I light the flames
to signal her arrival. Now she comes
as if the wind has carried her. At dusk,
mirrored, prevailing on the faded light
to linger now a moment while her steps

dancing in harmony to unheard notes
across the lacquered bridge spanning a stream
I cannot cross, past lions cut in stone
past every blossom, glowing in the last
remembrance of an afternoon that held
only the promise of her promenade

now realized as presence at my gate.
This candlelight, those flames, that swirling cloth
dancing their elegance through smoke, renew
my vision as her form arrives, and warms
my fascinated conjurings, designed
to charm the ecstasy of wind around

the interlacing of responsive limbs
as if a breath of air could make us burn
like incense, and the smoke enter our skin,
or swirling as a vortex in her source,
could be transposed to me as confluence
and given back as alm for her return.

Voyage de Noces

This unfamiliar azure, with its waves
flowing at dawn and evening to the east
where hills are maps of recent hurricanes
whose briefest passions are the august wind
and nights are luminescent swells beneath
the masted lights of other voyagers

gives way within me, as I watch her turn
towards a lost meridian, unmarked
on any map, but known to both of us
as former demarcation of a coast
unlike this southern shore where reefs converge
just past the water's edge, and as she walks

up from the sand into plumerias
arching above her almost dancing limbs
their rose a complement to indigo
around her shoulders as the garden moves
almost in time with her, in wind blown waves
concordant to the motions of the sea

behind her as she crests the coral path
crossing contesting shadows of capped terns
her hat weaving the sunlight on her skin,
I rise to greet her on the terrace as
voices of birds converge in harmonies
above us and we drift into the shade.

II
ATTACHMENT

"Sir, she is mortal;
But by immortal providence she's mine…"
~ Ferdinand

Sir Frederick Leighton (1830-1896). *The Painter's Honeymoon*, 1864.

Revery

Her veil, lifting, overcomes my gaze,
as if the smoke that flutters in the air
like bird wings on October wind, contrives
to mimic the complexities of stars,
or now renews the auguries who bore
signs of a different era in the dusk.

Her feet, on varnished floors, convince my ears
of mysteries untangled through a dance,
or, crossing polished marble, where each step
diagonals toward my langour, bends
my reveries within the sphere of light
she conjures in her undulated breath.

But in the jurisdiction of her voice
I am mute witness, having heard the notes
I acquiesce to bare complexities
of ornaments remade in reverence
and abdicating my seclusion rise
to purchase my conviction through her song.

and so the stolen constellated veil
whereon the dance is illustrated by
the sentence of orchestral harmonies:
her song is my restraint, that gently binds
together in secluded minuet
our figures as if drawn across the stars.

Renewal

My love becomes another when I take
her in my arms, or rather she renews
what she has always been: her reckless song
seems like the consciousness that birds prolong
each morning from the forest's rustic pews,
the colored splendor of a skillful voice

inflected by the wind, and I rejoice
in listening a moment, as she turns
to me, and changes: all her mysteries
are opened through enchanted expertise
and as each long remembered form returns
I bear her up, in harmony, her form

mirrored in images that, unwrapped, warm
even the frozen sinews I had thought
grown weak from lethargy, and I rejoice
within the confines of her gentle voice
and celebrate the figures she has wrought
within my mind, remembering the dawn

and transformations she has undergone
as flames become a moment silhouettes
that we may read as patterns of our will
or of imaginings, and yet they still
reshape themselves from wings into rosettes
refigured in my mind for her love's sake.

Lotus

And she, this morning, in my arms became
all things at once, my breath was hers within
the interwoven entwined space we shared.
She was the blossom and she was the bird,
a bed of crocus opening at dawn,
angles of geese in patterns on the wind.

I know, through touching hers, both cherry limbs
I saw as I came home against the sky
and buds swelling to petals at their tips
are within her and gathering around
at once the opening, fullness, and spent
I know each moment separately, and one

eternal moment, unified in her
as when December wind stopped, and all time
was then and now: her voice, her breath, her hand
the first moment of timelessness surprised
my thoughtless mind to waking, I embraced
her then, for now, for yesterday, and saw

whatever we can know of harmony
my flesh her food, her life my strength
our song my breath, but most of all the wind
moving around her as we move entwined
like crocus petals, cherry boughs or wings
or lotus blossoms moving in the sun.

Anacostia

Since spring has come, I walk the riverwood
at midday, and around me all is song
and blossoming, although last summer's thorns
half broken by the winter's snows remain.
I pick my way between them to the bank
eroded by old storms, and linger there.

Across the water, on the other shore
in sunlight, crocus bloom, and small white stars
blaze through short leaves of grass. I almost wish
I could cross over, but the current's filled
with broken limbs. I lie down near the edge
half dreaming of another distant place.

Just then I see them: dancing through the woods
to unheard music, lightly dressed, and one
among them sings. Although I cannot hear
a note, I feel the song beneath my skin
and wish only to cross the stream, to dance
in harmony with them to her bright song

but submerged thorns prevent our unity.
I look, and now they're gone. Am I awake?
Are those the voices of contending birds?
How can I know what happens on that shore
across from here? I rise, and moving north
plunge back into the shadows of the woods

Adornments

Miraculous your subtle nakedness
this morning, and your undulations near
our window, with their grace, deceived me to
misled conclusions of great harmony.
I followed them into the briars, where
thorns scratched my too authentic skin, and lost

whatever thread I had been following:
I watch your light form, unadorned, but love
the artifice of whispers even more
accoutrements of silk against your skin
or bangles, bought to please you as you dance
across the room, tempting exteriors

are complement to what you bare within
and if the light is prismed on your arm
or if your lips are redder than the earth
the jewelled tones enliven me, as I
enthralled, move to your calculated song:
for my devotion, rapturous in your

planned artifice, reacts to harmony
not to the thing, nor to its complement
but to their interplay, the lace between
your limbs is interwoven by design
just as your rings encircle all of me
if only in received imaginings.

Prey

Open your eyes. The beast prepares to feed
her sightless eyes now burning heatless coals
cleansing her heart and yours, taut skin more red
than any bronzework cauldron, where the dead
allow their weary, frayed, contorted souls
to brew together, liquor distilled here

and drunk in ritual by torchlight, clear
and sweeter to the huntress than her name
on those eternal lips. Now her mouth tears
your shoulder's flesh, as, wailing, she declares
accustomed ecstasy renewed, the same
each time for her, but only once for you,

her chosen quarry, grounded. There are few
she deigns to hunt, the antlered stag, gazelle
of forests, taken carefully, by swift
motions of ceremony, now a gift
to meet the hunger spelled voices compel
and only she can hear. Your role? Provide

her sustenance, until frenzies subside:
until she's sated, and the harsh caress
begins to slow. The song within her breath
gives you to understand this little death
is like rebirth. There's always more. She'll bless
each wound, and touch them, as they, healing, bleed.

Mayday

This forest should be all our thought today
how, from this window, in the early sun
those shadows reach across the floodplain where
we've seen the rushing overflow converge
bearing both trunk and crown along that stood
a decade on the bank, where now the buds

of rhododendrons clamour to the light
their scarlet promises still red before
the morning sun relights them, and the wings
of unnamed birds, unsettled by some sound
we cannot hear, weave patterns on the limbs
of sycamores that hide more than we know

and here, inside, I contemplate the scene
watching in mirrors as we fabricate
or create motion, Love, whose form is all
my thought at once, like forests or the new
constraints of presence, in whose hold you bend
like Daphne, who as birch limb I could hold

almost in motion still, and whose light voice
in singing called me forth as remedy
to stand a moment and remake the scene
in mirrors, constantly renewed, which I
constructed as a gift to you, and placed
within our rooms as vision of this day.

Mysteries

Her eyes are open as she walks across
this cluttered room, while shedding half her clothes:
that rocking chair becomes a hanger for
the pleated skirt I love, her earrings fall
onto a cabinet I once carried in
and placed beside her bed. She's singing now

a hymn I once reworked the lyrics for
at her request, but in this voice they live
a different circumstance than I'd foreseen:
in light prismatic tones enlivened by
the undefined transcendence of her womb.
Then placing my bent hands around her waist

I pull her back into the bed I made
again at her behest and shared design
in consummation of her votive will.
Unbuttoning the remnants of her guise
I touch this silent skin in whispers made
on these occasions for her soft delight

and she responds by bidding secret winds
to move around us: I can feel within
her limbs an energy I hadn't known
existed, feel her transfer it to me
enlivening my breath, and then I give
it back to her as recompense of love.

Restoration

A single candle serves. A small lamplight
will do, if burning: you must have a flame
somewhere nearby. And water – a small bowl
is best: it's through the waters we're made whole.
She must be there to whisper, or to name
what you remember, see, or come to know

within the ritual, and guide the flow
of what arrives, give energy its sound
and give light voice. Cast circles, near the bed,
of salt or petals help elation spread
or focus it: with luck, it may surround
both her and you, like streams of incense smoke

swirling in quiet air while you invoke
all you've forgotten: names, aromas, hymns,
the languages your spirit understands
and she still speaks. Then gently, with calm hands,
unclasp her fastenings, caress her limbs,
let her dress fall unheeded. Now explore

whatever curve she wills, the graceful shore
of her round breast, the harbor of her thighs
and she must do the same, until that grace
you half recall illuminates her face
as she becomes eternal, and your eyes,
which had been blind with loss, regain their sight.

Revision

I lose myself each eventide and must
build back the scaffolding. A crescent wrench
suffices for both pipes and rotten wood
at dawn. These noises are misunderstood
as intricate resettlings. I clench
all thought and figures in a clamp, and gaze

at random fittings, twisted in a maze
I long to resurrect with each new sun.
There's music in my head: a scattered tune
rewoven into hieroglyph or rune
unsoundable by modern ears, begun
in haste, and finished with the rushing night,

then saved as relic. It is my delight
to see their images as follies, where
unghostly forms, in moonlight, fall to trance
or to my rustic offerings advance
in unison, as if a crystal stair
awaited their cavorting. Remade hymns

light all the shadows of their revelled limbs
and echo in my head before I sleep
or haunt the patterns of my darkness, slow
these winds, before they gather, and bestow
destruction on this edifice, then sweep
these dancers, and their melodies, to dust.

On Learning How to Read

I read on summer evenings. Reclined,
consulting ancient stories of the birth
of everything around us, I consume
the explanations handed down by those
who may have known the origins of time
or heard the fables of its provenance

before the scribes miscopied them to scrolls.
She does not read. She sings. Entrancing songs
are remade here in candlelight. Her voice
across the room renews an antique hymn
as she, undressing, almost chants. Her shawl
soon drapes the rocking chair, her other clothes

describe a path towards the unmade bed
as incantations sanctify the room,
and hearing many voices, I remind
myself all come from her, an assonance
of notes across the centuries, a rhyme
first heard in firelight when half the earth

seemed animate, and voices could enthrall
their listeners to silence. I rejoice
as she renames the half-forgotten souls
in almost silent whisperings, her slim
form moves into my arms as she prolongs
the living melodies I'd only read.

Songe

She dreams of houses she had never known
or if she'd known them, dreams of hidden rooms
she never had imagined while she lived
beneath the curved, familiar roof. Within
their walls, sometimes, in hidden cabinets,
she finds lost objects: wands or rosaries

or bracelets whose inscriptions have been worn
through years of use to nothing readable.
And yet, while fingering their surfaces,
she still remembers what was written there
and hears the words within her mind, as if
no time had passed since each of them was lost,

as if the voice who read them first to her
were audible again, and present, as
she closes now the clasp around her wrist,
and rediscovering the joy she knew
when she first put it on, she starts to sing
within her dream, but in this darkened room

beside her, I can somehow hear her song,
and listening, can almost see her arm
encircled by a gold inscription, as
closing the drawer, she turns to me, and light
surrounds her as she walks, in memory,
or in this room we've built together here.

La Belle

An ordinary morning: as she wakes
still dressed in last night's evening clothes
she turns, remembering
whatever she had conjured, heat or dust
the half draped mirrors of her home
in revery transformed

and turns to me, whose fever all night warmed
whatever she conceived within
her solitary dream
ice blossomed forests, shorelines, cobalt seas
figures across a fallen bridge
expecting whispered words

from me, invoking flourishes of birds
as prologue, while uncovered skin
renews our harmonies
as I reveal every secret rose
her body offers, touch the ridge
outside her slender hips

caress the lavender between her lips
my voice fades to a quiet stream
feeding a gentle lust
and while my fingers, slowing, lightly comb
her trembling warmth, she starts to sing
just as the long wave breaks.

Rasa

My mind is always autumn when I think
of how her voice remade the golden trees
and the long wind that swept away the blue
declined sunlight renewed through prisms in
her melodies reminding me of lost
reflections from an inland sea restored

in mindfulness to harmonies inferred
by her reshaping of the ancient words
that I had somehow missed in studying
the monuments of bronze those singers raised
against whatever cold invaded their
imaginings of slow communion when

these same winds and their distant trees inclined
together to remake the earth in times
no spell could ever conjure: only in
the blessed songs and incantations hid
the revelations she brought forth in me
that afternoon, and onwards since that time

in every moment since I hear her voice
in every wind inflections of her song
and I remember, even as I walk
how her song lifted, fell, and rose again
and I am carried on, as if by wind
by that one instant remade for my life.

Spinning Yarns

I whisper in her ear each morning songs
for her delight, long fabrications, words
conveyed to focus all her thought on one
luxurious and long forgotten goal.
It keeps me centered, words and hands converge
in long designs of intrigue and slow love.

The feedback returns quickly: in her breath
are hints of useful words and gracious tropes
her skin my audience and instrument
flush if my whispers touch what's underneath
warm to my fingers as the story runs
along the lines we've known for centuries:

in ancient times, the women at their looms
or at their spinning wheels reminisced
or reinvented anecdotes to charm
hours away, how mermaids came to shore
or how defiant captives came to know
new homes, and remade everything they found

and in the background, shuttles lightly crossed
taut strings, and interwoven fingers held
spaces apart, the pattern endlessly
repeated then, and now, in my own voice
designed to please her memories and bring
her closer to me in this warming room.

Miranda

Since that first fall along the shoreline I've
called her my jewel all these years although
she often spoke with certainty of glass.
She's kept a garden journal, and today
was the latest frost of all we've ever known:
most of the autumn blossoms have survived–

I don't know how she does it and don't ask.
Some mysteries are best left unexplained,
like how one touch can fill my limbs with strength
as if we were, well, two and twenty, but
almost naïve in love. Last night, against the cold
we slept in darkness, interlaced, her skin

warm against mine, as each night for years
and each night new: another pattern– spline
or herringbone, it is her second gift.
She sings, I write, we garden, sometimes dance
in interwoven movements, scarves and silk,
like pearls never lost. Mysterious

this morning by the lower pond, I held
a sheet of sudden ice, thin as a pane
and nearly clear, but looking close, I saw
small bits of air encased, and looking through
saw then her face in sunlight– jeweled silk
around her shoulders– looking through at me.

Landscape

Outside, the irises are withered blades.
Birdsong is all within. I play the loop
anticipating what I know is warmth
about to give itself to counter winds.
Our only gemstone colors are her skirt
in lamplight, and her falling cobalt scarf.

It seems enough, as darkness wraps itself
around the broken lattices of brick
surrounding us. The leafless willows bend
by my design, along the staggered fence
and I can hear our stairstepped mortar catch
the first flakes of this winter reconciled

to what will seem an endless recompense
since in their melting, they predict the frost
arranged in triangles on windowpanes
and lingering within my sight for weeks.
It's better to resign myself to red
emphatic flannel for a season, trimmed

with ivory lace, since, underneath, her form
may still retain the fervor of the spring
that feeds those irises, and frames the blue
reflections of a distant tone her voice
invents, almost as if the wind, through song,
could cause my blossoming within her arms.

III
HEARTHSONGS

"… Marquis, there is a vast difference between merely enjoying happiness and relishing the sensation of enjoying it."
~Ninon de L'Enclos

Herbert James Draper (1863-1920).
Water Baby, 1890.

Flow

I watch the tiny shorebirds interweave
their flight into a knotted flock, as swells
roll in, and gather, break, each one a new
revision of the last, moving the air
only enough to lift delicate wings
at perfect angles over sudden breaks

and as I watch, their movements and the waves
begin to merge, and flow in unison
as if all elements together wove
their patterns endlessly within our minds
and losing note of time become the gaze
that fixes motion as a single point

but suddenly the beach horses arrive
searching our bags for food, at fourteen hands
slight as lost apparitions, present here
by processes of mystery or myth
they move along the shore in reverie
unhurried, interrupted by the wind

and slowly, slowly fade from sight. Those birds
have grown more numerous, their complex skeins
redoubled, while the waves renew their course
and I return to contemplation as
the shadows cast by wings are lengthening
until they seem the corresponding sea.

St. Thomas

Tide pools. Sunlight. Shorebirds overhead.
Young James constructing at the waterline
his narrative of voyaging across
this azure to those islands we can see
only at dawn and dusk: the tradewinds draw
curtains of salt across our eyes at noon.

I stand with three iguanas on a rise
among plumerias whose petals move
from white to rose to crimson when they fall
and line volcanic landscapes in long drifts
their contrast sheer against the breakers white
transversal of our broken coral reef

the clarity of sapphire renews
itself after each swell and circulates
in guided currents unknown butterflies
and predatory angels scattering
those nets of luminescent fins. I walk
down to the sands just as she rises up

and we walk out together on the rocks
as James watches, his thoughts of voyage lost
until the urchins spear her foot. She leaps
into my arms, and I still have the strength
to bear her back to shore, as seabirds weave
their shadows on the unrelenting shore.

Reflections

This morning, a young boy, in sleepy haste
knocked down his mirror: from another room
I heard the shattering of images
and went to look: there, scattered on the floor
rough shards reflected sunlight and green limbs,
hints of swift flights of wrens an instant as

they dove contesting past unbroken panes,
and as we gathered them each caught a scene
one slivered instant, then moved on, but I
remembered something I'd seen years ago:
a man had made a wooden box, and lined
the whole interior with mirrored glass

and as he closed it in the sunlight I
imagined bearing it to a dark room
and loosing there the captured light within,
as when I gazed upon my love, who sat
before her mirror, brushing out her hair
in candlelight, and watched her eyes reflect

the luminescent flame in resonance
to her light breath, and breathing as I watched
I caught within my mind her portrait, held
it while she walked to me in whispers so
I could return it here, if only in
these evanescent coruscated words.

Return

Two deer graze underneath those windmill trees
as James and I go by. We stop. One's head
rises from browsing, looks. The other turns
towards us, then away. Her tail flips
a pulse of white, and quickly she recedes
into the undergrowth, and then she's gone.

Someone comes up behind us. We move on.
I glance back, and the first is staring still
along our path. James notices, and seems
as if he'd linger, fascinated by
her motionless but animated form,
but we turn for our destination now.

I drop him at the door. He makes me vow
we'll soon return to that catalpaed hill
as if we could remake the time, transform
some future moment back, renew the seeds
of what he felt, and cultivate the slips,
the cuttings of emotion, reinvent

the feelings of that instant we had spent
to make them bloom again. And I would try
to populate the landscapes of his dreams
with leaves that deer could browse when she returns,
but know exactly why she, silent, fled
and have no words to remake what he sees.

Le Vin du Diable

Our graduation ceremonials
are marked in fermentations, moving from
the bottled ciders of our teenagers
at family gatherings, towards Champagne
on coming home from universities.
And each year I am called on to explain

the process of its fabrication, how
the grapes are grown, and where. Dom Pérignon
did not invent the process. It was first
discovered by an Englishman, who gave
a paper on the method. Sugared yeast
is added to the once fermented wine

but it was Pierre Pérignon, a monk,
who fabricated wired corks that held
the second fermentation still. Three years
is often necessary. Turned in racks
meticulously till it's ready, lees
disgorged, and dosed sometimes with aged Cognac

or framboise and resealed, it arrives
as labored wine. Almost as sacrament,
in handmade flutes by candlelight, we toast
the years in rites of passage, rituals
whose words, selected carefully, convey
the laboured art of generations grown.

Victimae Paschali Laudes

We walk in, barely late. The choir ends.
He's got an apple, half consumed. She says
"He can't eat that in here." I hand it to
his brother, who's embarrassed. For a while
all goes in peace. There's song and sermon, then
the singer sits a moment with us all.

But soon she's off, and he just can't hold still.
I take him to the back: the crying room
where those as him are suffered. Once inside
he finds a door direct out to the sun.
Of all the things: he wants to climb a tree!
and from there points at birds: two mourning doves

along the walk, a starling gathering
straw for his nest. He flies up to the eaves.
A poor man near the church door asks for alms
but I have none. Those doves are flying past
the main door, where a woman staggers out.
She's leaning on her mother. All around

uncles and brothers mill, concerned. A new
tree beckons while the ambulances come.
They bear the woman off. He says, "When I
am dead they'll carry me away like that."
He's four years old. We go inside, but she
has driven on to sing another Mass.

Disorder

Last Saturday, I took James for a walk.
He's four, and moody. Sometimes he just needs
to burn some energy. The forest, wet
with still more rain arriving, waved its boughs
and from the bridge we watched the western bank
crumble into the current, one more tree

falling across the span. We headed back
and our whole yard, between spring wind and dogs
and James himself, was wreckage: garden hoes
and ski poles, broken pottery, a few
cut logs dragged up the hill for some lost game
and left there to roll halfway down again:

it seemed too much. I carried him inside
and staggered up the stairs, whose banister
was missing more than one upright: they made
in his imagination, rapiers
against stray dinosaurs. Down the long hall
baskets of lingerie confused our path

and hymnals blocked the door. I pushed right through
and there she was, still working. All around
her swirled programs, sheets of music, stacks
of ancient scores, and she, the vortex of
all chaos, sang an ordered song so sweet
I acquiesced to measured harmonies.

Misunderstanding

Our spring comes late this year: those peregrines
have not returned to steeples, daffodils
of all things in late march are blooming still.
And past my birthday, cherries still in bud
are only hinting of a distant land.
What can we make of time? Can we depend

on nothing? Two wrens nested in my shop
last year, and they returned at Valentine's.
I haven't seen them since. Our river flows
inside its banks, reflecting cherry bark
on croci, if we linger. Wandering
with Easter coming on, I try to speak

but what if words like earthsigns are confused?
I've spent a lifetime learning them. Today
I planted freesias, while the cardinals
whistled their scarlet songs across the frost,
and thought of home. The equinox is past
and we, who once had sung of coming times

are almost voiceless. Now, the iris should
be greeting us at dawn, and mockingbirds
should have disturbed our nights for weeks. This sky
is filled with unknown light at evening, or
with misread signs. I know. I placed them there
hoping you'll find them, hoping you will know.

Wrenhouse

I've made a life of losing everything.
This morning, with my coffee, I looked out
and saw the wrenhouse shattered. When a storm
blew down a cherry limb, I'd taken up
my saw and made a turning blank. The lathe
revolved it gently as a form emerged

and James, excited, asked if he could stay.
I made him sit up on the workbench. When
he waved his arms, I ordered him to keep
his fists thrust into pockets, as I'd done
in my own father's shop when I was four.
He wanted to help sand. I turned it off

and let him run glass paper over wood.
The lacquer flowed on smoothly, and we hung
the whole thing from a tree limb by the deck.
It looked medieval. It looked like it came
from mythic forests, peopled with strange sights.
The wrens soon claimed it. I checked every day

and felt some sadness when they'd raised their clutch
then flew together north in unison.
The birdhouse hung there isolate, and now
this morning, I found pieces of its roof.
whatever I construct soon shatters. Why
must everything continually fall?

Visionary

Look there: the forest, leafed now with its green
exuberance of budding lobes renews
itself and us whenever we can gaze
with something like clear eyes on all its forms
holding a moment in our sight, as if
instants could last forever if we look

closely enough: once, in a blizzard I
descended a long slope much like this hill
while snow clung to the windward side of boughs
contrasting with rough bark of sycamores
and saw her, brushing drifts away in blue-
her scarf a wave of silk on the white shore-

or once, in January, when the clear
new wind had swept its coldest air across
the polished granite of a harbored bench
and she, in chiseled sunlight, clear as glass
her sharp outlines defined by scrimshawed scenes
leaned forward, as her jewelled eyes engaged

my own a moment, burned to memory:
if we walk now into this midspring wood
where oak and locust merge their woven leaves
creating hidden shade, and if she turns
a moment towards me in her gold thread blouse,
grant me clear eyes to hold her in my mind.

Storm

June hurricanes are coming on again:
somewhere at sea, in latitudes unknown
but east of here, and south, a spiraling
column of air, within a thunderstorm
is seed to still unmeasured turbulence
and even now, small birds are carried on

and changed to ice at thirty thousand feet
then dropped into the waves. Long whitecaps form
away from shore, unnoticed, gathering
the hidden strength of cyclones at their peaks
as laden wind turns back upon its rings
and layers on the thundered violence

to any who can bear it. My love speaks
in measured tones, along this coast, whose heat
begins to build each morning, hovering
above our forest, in resplendent shades
of green and gray, its leaves already blown
into loose patterns, lightly circling

in premonition of approaching wind
and broken limbs to come, their twisted braids
of bark sewing the river shut some dawn
a week from now, or two, yet my love sings
not of those floods or broken trunks, but boughs
that may remain, if our bent wind allows.

Prayer

I know these mountains: above timberline
their naked rocks and crumbling sands give way
beneath the sudden thunders on the ridge
where snowmelt mixes with the flashing rain
to swell the creeks in unison, and rush
their waters down the unrestrained ravines

towards chaotic valleys, where the trees
first thrust up from the accidented earth:
kingdoms of tangled branches and torn vines.
There in the streambed, rocks cascade the flow
of rushing water, tumbling near the banks
or glistening in sunlight near those few

breaks in the canopy. But suddenly
a streambank widens on the valley floor
the waters stop their churning, and a calm
spreads out across a vast lake, deep and still
reflecting unimaginable skies
of blue and white infinitude before

a long climactic waterfall, and there
the moment ends, or replicates: all birds
return, and ferns wave in the overspray.
Again, again: it's mesmerizing here
where time has stopped if only briefly and
our words are whispered to declining wind.

Jewelweed

Our forest isn't much for rattlesnakes,
or even copperheads, their patterned backs
red diamonds beneath last autumn's leaves.
It's small things here that get you: devil's thorn
raking bare flesh, deer ticks or lenten rose,
and poison ivy clambers every patch

along the meadow's edge. I pull by hand
thin running stems wherever they invade,
careful to keep the leaftips from my skin.
This spring our rains have favored jewelweed
whose coral blossoms draw the rubythroats.
I leave a few to grow since their juice makes

a balm for poison ivy, which relieves
the subtle burning if applied within
a quarter hour. Knowing this, Baird planned,
at nine, immunity from more attacks
of blistering, and taking off his clothes
rubbed poison ivy everywhere. He'd made

a poultice, just in case, but could not match
the poison to its antidote. Forlorn,
confessed and bathed, at dinner he'd concede
unwisdom, but years later, he still notes
that even well-planned traumas test belief
but partial cures flourish near every grief.

IV
CONSTRUCTING BEAUTY

"Plus me plaît le séjour qu'ont bâti mes aïeux,
Que des palais Romains le front audacieux,
Plus que le marbre dur me plaît l'ardoise fine...."
~Du Bellay

John William Godward (1861-1922).
At the Garden Shrine, Pompeii, 1892.

Talavera

First have a plan in mind. A crowbar will
help pop out the old counter and remove
all useless trim. The cabinets come apart
quite easily, and after, you can start
to strip your drywall to the studs. Improve
the framing lumber, if you dare. Remake

the outlets while they're open, and resnake
the disassembled pipes. Now reinstall
the cabinets and lay new plywood out
in double layers. Try to do without
too many screws slant angled to the wall.
Now lay your tiles out. You'll need a graph

to mark the place of each. A measured staff
will aid alignment later. Place accents
as sparingly as possible. Now stir
the thinset carefully. You may prefer
to spread it in small patches. This prevents
too rapid drying. Working quickly, place

each precut piece into its marked out space
adjusting for irregularities
and press them home. A dampened rag will serve
to wipe away loose grout, and still preserve
the surface. There's no special expertise
involved, patience makes up for lack of skill.

Hinges

Good mortises are difficult. The grain
must be respected. Marking gauges trace
a better line than you can draw by hand,
and outlining will always leave a space.
Only sound templates stay repeatable
but must be stored with care. Before we met

I never once installed a metal hinge
correctly. I would hold the finished gate
in place with jams or wedges, and then drill
with any handy bit, three pilot holes
or simply drive the screws without regard
for any complications. Barreled pins

would hold a year or two. It seemed enough.
But now I build for permanence. Her eyes
are watching, even when they're not. The depth
is tested for perfection, well before
I set a chisel to the finished wood.
These templates are preserved for future use

and not just by my hands. This workshop shelf
secures what any carpenter would need
to reproduce the fair curve of a door
that passed inspection of her eyes and hands
or went unnoticed as she lightly used
the products of my careful laboring.

Mousetrap

Darkness, sometime near three, when we both wake
to scratching claws somewhere close by the bed.
I try to scare it first, pound on the walls
and all seems calm, but soon noises return.
No chance of sleep now. I must rise, and find
whatever draws the scraping to this room.

There must be something for it to consume
beneath the wardrobe? Underneath the shelves?
I sweep it all in lamplight, find more things
than I'd imagined possible. Near dawn
at last the silence lingers. I will need
benevolent new traps. At noon, I drive

to look for something it will, caught, survive,
without new suffering laid on my head.
Though she, in weary supplication, calls
for any remedy, my whole concern
is peace for everyone: all those consigned
to this haphazard place. There's no pain here:

I place the quarter round contraptions near
our routed trim. We settle in ourselves,
each in our spot, and wait. The midnight brings
more scratching, as the mouse is gently drawn
by scented bait, caught, borne outside, and freed
not knowing it had been my love at stake.

Arts and Mysteries

We walk the Vermont landscape looking for
a likely tree. I find one near the stream
her brother and I fell it. Chainsaw noise
reduces it to rounds and fire wood.
I sling two circles in the pickup bed
and three days later pull out, heading south.

One winter Friday evening I took up
a round, and halved it, placed it on the lathe
as slow as I could make it turn, then made
the shape, and crafted out a foot, refixed
the form, and hollowed it into a bowl
then sanded, sanded, shellacked it, and left

it drying till the morning, when we drove
to Crozet, and while she knocked on the door
I waxed the finish, buffed, and whispered "done."
We gave it to her aunt, who had grown up
sometimes on that same landscape in Vermont
and now walked quiet pathways. But I've learned

that nothing's ever done: the finish bled.
We took it home with us and promised her
I'd use tung oil. It took three months: I rush
or slowly, patiently, resolve the sheen
or sometimes I do both, as with some gifts
that take more years than I can count to learn.

Passionate Virtuosity

It's not enough to twine these copper strands
together into spirals, not enough
to bend them into hooks, and slowly twist
setscrews down tight: their torquing strains my wrist,
but holds them as I push outlets through rough
sawn openings and switch the breaker on.

I still must test this saffron Romex drawn
through half-inch holes I'd drilled in treated sides
of cabinets and tacked with wire clips.
It's best to pound these solid. If one slips
the whole island will darken. Nothing hides
these bent and coiling shapes, but who would see?

I call her down to look. It works, but she
objects to how the cable's held in place.
It won't affect the way the burners heat
but she still wants it changed, made more discreet,
neatly reworked. There's no appeal. Grace
demands silent acceptance. Molded track

formfit and cut to span along the back
of every cabinet takes a whole day
but even I, who had to reconnect
each outlet in the run, and reinspect
the grounded circuits in their new array,
admit the beauty of her firm demands.

Sovereignty

Beyond the house, beyond the fence I built
last summer, down the slope I cleared with saws
and brushhooks, past the sycamore too large
for any blade I have, with its hung vines,
beyond the trilliums, immaculate
with white each April, vanishing by June,

I cleared the loose dimensions of a glade,
cut saplings down, untangled every vine,
rank poison ivy, devil's thorn, red grape,
tore out coarse undergrowth and carried limbs
storm fallen, to the bramble edge, then mowed
our meadow grasses almost to a lawn.

I'd hoped to make a ground for summering,
for play and evening song, perhaps a spot
where she could mark up scores in quietude
untroubled by the chaos of the house,
but lifting up the last decaying wood
disturbed a swarm of hornets. Poisoned barbs

winged everywhere. I felt them through my shirt
and stripped it as I ran. My other clothes
littered a path towards the riverbank
where finally I paused, my skin in flames.
Doused in the stream, I called out, then returned
to gather what was left, and limped inside.

Prosody

In silent concert hastening along
our redwood planks, brown, mined by rampant bees
and halfsawn in odd places by the hands
of William James, a wren, astonished, stands
attempting to make sense of what he sees:
three unaccustomed figures near his nest

dining in quietude. His mate's protest
pushes his flitting caution past the breach
and three quick hidden voices force his wings
to open, bearing him and all he brings:
a few cut worms, one meant to quiet each
cajoling tongue. Delivered, he escapes

back to the shadowed canopy. Our shapes
are free to move, and we, speechless, observe
the vanishings of other wings, her blurred
ascension through the birch tangles obscured
in harmony with his, the subtle curve
of flight hiding intent. In quick reply

he bends his track to hers. They both defy
our unfamiliar motionless design
with raucous intonations, then explore
the undersides of limbs and leaves before
voices return from woven twigs, combine
in choral blend, and reinvent our song.

Censer

Cleaning my shop, I find a strip of lath
used by my son for burning stick incense–
a gentle arc, and grooved, with one hole drilled
at each curved end. The finish marred by burns,
a few knife marks still visible, it's light
as any memory, light as lost smoke.

And I remember watching as long chains
advanced along the pews, remember clouds
rising above our heads, and purple robes
walking through chants to stone. The broken edge
reflected our stained light of leaded glass,
marble transformed by prisms through still air.

But more than that: my preparations done,
after the candles all were lit, and cloth
was draped to make the shadows seem as wings
moving within imagined wind, I struck
a match, and sulfur filled the room before
she walked undraped into the clouded air.

And after all the candles had burned down,
only the glow of incense still remained.
The air then filled with prayers, her voice and mine,
and yet another listened: was it smoke
or something else, cast bronze or sanded wood
still carving shadows, shaped almost as lath?

Ritual

I built each feature of this empty room
with my own hands, this desk, even these walls,
and painted everything a gleaming white
knowing the risks, believing I'd invite
through action, peace. And now, as evening falls
the two of us, defeated, need to cleanse

this space again. I've studied, and her friends
have given us the implements we need:
salt from a sacred sea, candles, incense,
water she thinks of as a strong defense,
a piece of blessed cloth, and one small seed
reaped silently by cherished hands. I spread

the salt into a circle near the bed
we place ourselves within and light the flame,
then I incant the words I've learned, and pour
a little water, gently, to the four
directions, speaking slowly the lost name
and calling for protection for all those

who still remain with us. The candle throws
its steady light around the circle, she
repeats my words in chanting, and we hold
our hands together, hoping to enfold
all those we love in lasting harmony
as incense folds us in its meshed perfume.

Jouissance

Our August forest blossoms, but these trees
have shed some leaves, enough to half expose
this symmetry of branches, and their known
consanguinate complexities are shown
in harmony at last, the verdant clothes
fallen away, or scattered to extremes:

they drift to our back fence, where young James dreams
the earth has been created just for him:
the playhouse I once built with my own hands
and we by choice have painted white, still stands
against all summer storms with its red trim
reflected in his splashing pond. Deck stairs

have been shored up, and I've enameled chairs
to ebony, by her command, who stirs
inside the kitchen I've half-finished, broth,
while wearing the articulated cloth
I've given her, the pearls she prefers
gleaming in lamplight as she bids me taste

the fabricated offerings, her waist
enticing me to other joys, unknown
before I heard her song, whose intricate
measures confirm eternal delicate
relations in their slender, jeweled tone:
the rhythms she renews to, gently, please.

Constructing Beauty

It only happens to the fallen. Trees
blown down in August hurricanes
or broken by icestorms
are chainsawn into shortgrain rounds. Their bark
is grinder stripped. Bandsaws reduce
the whole to halves. Their dust

will cloud your sight. Work through it. Bolt the plate
onto the plane, and start your lathe.
Watch as it gathers speed
for asymmetric patterns. Touch the grind
to rest, and gently lever chips
until you form a sphere.

Reverse the blank, and bolt it back. Now clear
all shadowmarks. The bowlgouge strips
away those intertwined
ridges inside. Once smooth, renew your bead
and push along the walls. Now shave
the rim until it's straight

and start sanding the turning bowl. You must
run through the grits, but introduce
some variance in forms
that others, turning edges, will remark
when serving what the bowl contains
forgetting expertize.

Château Miranda

Bent to cramped knees, a chisel in your hand
chipping away at grout or wonderboard
(to clean up two square damaged feet, and lay
replacement tiles now takes half a day
or so it seems, until ceramic's scored
and snapped, the mastic spread, trimmed corners set,)

consider broken castles. Don't forget
each of those ruined beams was hewn at length
by hands like yours, each marble rail shaped
a sixteenth with each stroke of bevel scraped
across gold crystal veins. It took such strength
and delicate exactness each curve meant,

between rhythms of planing and time spent
resharpening dulled blades, a week at best.
Now they lay shattered. Smashed rosettes, and squares
of tessellated amber litter stairs
pockmarked by sledges. Plaster, once distressed,
begins to crumble, falls. Its dust cascades

across the opalescent wrought brocades
of alabaster flooring, and conceals
each hardwon crafted edge. These ravaged halls
remind: even a wellset crescent falls,
and crosscut angles of mitered reveals
will quickly meet a stress they can't withstand.

V
ANTECEDENTS

"There have been lovers who thought love should be
So much compounded of high courtesy
That they would sigh and quote with learned looks
Precedents out of beautiful old books…"

~Yeats

John William Godward (1861-1922).
Lesbia with her Sparrow, 1916.

Raven

In ancient times, ten suns circled our land
and burned the crops. An archer came
to shoot nine down: they fell,
becoming ravens when they touched the earth.
The grateful gods bestowed on him
their immortality

but asked he meditate a year, to see
with their revealing eyes. He set
their gift aside and thought
of distant things: of us. And yet, his wife,
abandoned by his journey, stole
the gods' eternal gift

and fled on foot. The archer was too swift:
she had to hide. To save her life
those ravens called her name
and led her to a cave where she could dwell.
She was betrayed. She watched him swim
towards her hiding place.

The ravens urged her to become the face
we see now in the moon: she bought
in hiding her rebirth.
And still, at evening moonrise, they console
her loss with cries, and at moonset
our ears can understand.

Night Pearls

At first, I thought them legends: Warring States
romances make some mention. In the Spring
and Autumn Annals, sometimes we may read
of minerals whose crystal veinings bleed,
when warmed, fresh light in darkness, auguring
moonlight or dawn, but from within. If flame

is banned through caution or a festive game,
hallways may be illuminated by
cleft stones gathered in copper bowls, their rims
rolled down like silk. When luminescence dims
they need merely be heated. Hand or thigh
each serve as well for this. Imagine, then,

a necklace made of light blue crystals. When
placed on bare skin, those beads would start to glow
revealing everything: the room, these hands.
Bathing her breasts in radiance, the strands,
unknotting as she moves, may blaze up, throw
new patterns on taut limbs, lattice or lace

where eyes or hands may follow, fingers trace
or lips caress. Be careful now: the stones
if broken from their string, will strew these sheets
with blue, and darken if no blood warmth heats
their surfaces, but lucid undertones
may reappear in warmth their light translates.

Mirrors

On scales held by Aphrodite, weighed
against each other, brothers, with their bows
always at hand, contested for a palm
and have for years: Anteros tries to tear
the frond from Eros, who resists, as we
contend through love, here mirroring their fight

as if our loves were surrogate, our sight
clouded by dust they raise, and She, who should
protect us from their feud, closes her eyes,
as any understanding lover would,
confronted as she is by gold and lead.
She's crippled by calamity, and breaks

her heart and ours. Her sorrows, our mistakes,
in love are one. The letters we compose
on a stairwell, or in gardens, are misread,
no blossoms frame our messages, no balm
can salve our wounds, collateral, divine
and yet, continuing, we try to live

as if Her rapt attention could still give
some promise, help us cross the threshold, see
a whirlygig that carves the evening air,
as woodworkers carve spindles, and combine
splined forms into long sequences, devise
to keep us safe, an earthly palisade.

Melusine

Her breasts exposed, light handed, out of time,
bathing in wooden vessels as she sings
in distant languages I've never heard,
she draws my gaze. I cannot help but stare
as, laughing, she rubs oil on her skin,
then catches my long gaze without disguise,

as once her mother heard the rushing cries
of hounds, and looked up, caught. She gave her hand
only after his promises were sworn
and witnessed: that no man would ever look
on her when bathing. Years became decades
as hunter kept his quarry safe until

drunken temptation overcame his will
and he looked in. She treated sight as sin
and changed herself. His jeweled gifts, his rings,
his necklaces fell to the floor. No word
escaped her lips. Astonishment and scorn
her only offerings that night she fled

both husband and his wooden marriage bed,
raising her daughter in this foreign land
where I, by chance, see polished shells adorn
her breasts, white as the pages of a book
I long to read after our daylight fades
quickly, before the moon begins its climb.

Redemption

Our trees are blossoming. They almost burn
before their leaves appear. The petals blaze
in sunlight, even as the wind comes on
still cold as sacrificial gifts. They fall
eternally it seems, among the wings,
among the unmown stalks, among the weeds.

A peacock's voice is not like other birds
but still their feathers shine. The grackles raise
their own voices, like ours, with each new dawn
and even if their tails, stretched as fans
do not contain the multilayered suns
of peacocks, they're redeemed by the same light.

We're all the poor, and each of us, confined
within the limitations of a fence
common to all, is judged as symbol, like
those swans, ungainly as they make their way
towards some distant pond, as light becomes
the violent measurement of shadowed grace.

And so with her, who knew the season short:
who hoped distortion could illuminate
not just her sight, but each of ours, whose pride
had blinded us, just as the early sun
will blind the peacock into voiced displays
in fanned transplendence as the wind comes on.

Columbina

No mask: her blush the object of this scene,
her belladonna eyes and coral lips
tempt everyman. Forgetting half his age
he watches as she slip-dances across
the broken space between them. Half the stage
is hers, and as she sways those balanced hips
still certain he'll be watching, we can see

she holds the keys of every mystery
discovered through an accident of birth
or through constructed plans, whispered behind
stage curtains, palms, or smoke: the gain or loss
of every generation redefined
within her phrases, and the measured worth
of every suitor moderated here,

reduced to cadence by the smooth veneer
of unassuming speech: a few quick words
and careful ambuscades begin to fall,
the balustrades crumble. Who needs a gloss
when movements of her hands, controlled, recall
scenes from our lives, shadows, the flight of birds
whose sudden wings discover clandestine

suitors or servants who, exposed, begin
to confess all, as if they were compelled
by fear or love of her light form, by lust
coerced and purified, until the dross
is burned and blown away, as if the dust
revealed all our patterns or withheld,
in swirling chaos, half her craft unseen?

Sumeria

> "...and like a moonbeam she came forth to him..."
> ~The Sated Lover, c. 2500 BCE

Perhaps she was the daughter of the moon
I cannot say. I only know that men
reported, after revelries, she'd come
and take advantage of their drunkenness
to drag them off, beyond the city walls
and bid them plough her fields throughout the night.

And old men say she journeyed once beneath
the earth, finding a pathway past the gates
darkened by shadows of lost warriors.
At each portal the keeper made her give
away something brought down from our made earth:
A rod of lapis lazuli, the beads

around her neck, a golden torc, her dress
until she finally stood, completely bare
then challenged judges to pronounce their worst
and work their will. They did, but let her go:
thus she brought back the water and the bread
and bore the seasons back to us. It's said

that in her memory, for centuries
young women went to temple grounds and sat
once in their lives, until an unknown man
dropped coins into her cup. That was her sign
to drag him off, as she had, for one night
to consecrate those sacred grounds once more.

Spinning Wheel

Within my arms, her listening consumes
all light outside, all motion: in this dark
my voice is her whole work. The rising sound
leads everything she knows: an undertone
of deepened rhythm claims even her skin
wherever lacework moves above my hand.

And once, such stories told, where loose thread spanned
the distances of distaffs and great wheels
in rooms of women laboring the flax,
by one who sat among them through the day,
excited even retters as they spun
the rough fibers across their lips, and knew

the secrets of the land where Frigga grew
the first blue blossoms. Silent in the stark
turning of wheels, echoing on stone,
the stories kept them spinning, as the wax
burnt lower, and the legends turned around
their minds like thread around the straightened spokes,

as now, in this still room, my voice invokes
those same emotions, echoed. I begin
rough whispers, lengthened, drawn out, as she feels
woven connections raveled loose, undone
until her robe, in gentle disarray,
renews the secrets of constructed looms..

Gold

Near equinox red seeds hand scattered sprout
between perennials at her command
among the signatures of last year's herbs.
The rows, transformed to clouds, retain their green
only until the wind resumes: silver
the undersides of leaves, in dance, renew

all promises: ripe buds converge with blue
swelling inside, as if divinity
had chosen, as her color, just this shade
for any robe she wore. The watered earth,
her path and mine, now opening, displays
prefigured transformations dried beyond

all point of seeding, stalks, matured and blond
must still be gathered, dressed, and left unseen
beneath the summer surface, where new birth
is possible, only if she'll confer
her blessing through the chants each woman made
in other seasons, while sunshine or rain

combined together in the endless chain.
Then taken up, retted, and dried by hand
spun fine in rooms where no man's voice disturbs
the ancient cycles of a trinity
the thread's dyed gold with lichen, clover: praise
her bounty and their skill. Praise her devout.

Silk Road

The stage is blank now. Ribbons swirling, smoke
illuminated from beneath by red
lamps focused on the emptiness, oak boards
laid down into a pattern which affords
a place to leap and land: the colored thread
of narrative in dance has disappeared.

Those arms, like crane wings catching air, once sheared
the curtained wind as if to fly, their lines
as straight as quills, or intricate cleft braids
whose interwoven motion still cascades
like water falling through the wreathed designs
we only dreamed could be performed. But she

who danced with careless practiced ecstasy,
and gave movement to form, her legs taut springs
to carry her along those lights where birds
no longer fly, the calligraphs of words
written in air by limbs where red silk clings,
leapt into space and found no place to land.

We all must fall in pain. I understand.
But still I dream of cranes among the reeds,
their wings just opening, ready for flight,
extended feathers catching sunset light
like fingers parting strings of colored beads,
rising a little more with each wingstroke.

VI
GRACEFUL DESIGNS

"We think by feeling. What is there to know?
I hear my being dance…"
~Roethke

Pavel Petrovich Ivanov (Paul Mak) (1885-1960).
Schéhérazade with a Peacock, 1924.

Stone Cutters

We do it now with saws. Back then, a sledge
tapped pitching chisels straight along the face
before a granite ax confirmed the line.
You've seen broached work: its centers rough, the fine
borders made square and smooth– a kind of grace
in contrast lends itself to buttresses

for bracing walls. A crandall, swung, dresses
the block, and leaves it ready to be laid
into a pointed arch which bears the weight
above it. This design allowed the great
cathedrals to be built, whose walls displayed
rose windows made of spun glass and soft lead,

the cobalt oxides melted inside spread
sunlight through prismed streams: carmine and blue.
Those cutters, working stone, imagined tall
bar traces they would never see: that wall
would take two lifetimes. No one person knew
every detail: how the labyrinth

mirrored the sacred numbers, how the plinth
was settled into place. Each worked their part
alone, hoping carved pieces fit the whole
with seamless joints, resisting still, the slow
cracks of decay, or swift collapse of art,
where falcons, hunting, perch the hand cut edge.

Labyrinth

These tessalate lunations, vitrified
almost, by kiln and sunlight in our square,
now blue and white, were set by unknown hands,
and yet, to anyone one who understands,
provide a path to take, supply a rare
union of thought and act. Towards the rose,

not wandering– since quadrants interpose
themselves against diversion– discipline,
attention, care, and patience here convey
our steps when navigating this array.
We enter by a gate. The lines begin
to turn, and we must follow. Intersects

are unknown here, each curvature reflects
the last, and we move on at our own pace,
through quadrants, to the center, where we pause.
And at this center, contemplation draws
our thoughts away from unicursal space
a little time. But soon we must unwind

the selfsame path, here mirrored in our mind,
and on this pavement, whose design may teach
considered lessons of humility,
and give, through practiced steps, serenity,
remembering how once a patient speech
within a wine cellar, calmed the lost bride.

Glass Harmonica

These bowls, spindled, confuse. So painted red
for C, dark blue for A, their rims become
octaves, ethereal as any mist
distracting hand and ear. Their tones persist
in air as atmosphere. Players succumb
to madness, haunted by the earthless sound

of crystal rims, whose cutglass figures, round
half spheres, remind the listener of young
orchards in spring whose first fruit, understood
as sweet sap on the still unripened wood,
seems like the earliest of songs she'd sung:
unspoken promises, a glance, the small

light touch of whispers near a garden wall.
Or if her lover hears translucent notes,
they force return of dreams, remembered long
after the dawn's return, after birdsong
reshadows limbs, after the pipe-led goats
abandon orchard lawns, their revels done

except within his mind, as fingers run
along those rims, through octaves, as the air
harbors vibrations, resonating in
both listeners now, while the vessels spin
as she continues playing, unaware
of reminiscences her rhythms spread.

Theological College

Tulip magnolias through leaded glass:
handpoured, imperfect, rolled and cut
into its copper frames–
the spring courtyard in oblique bloom,
bent light remaking knotted shoots
before our equinox.

I pace the halls. A stained glass door unlocks
into the rebuilt sacristy
with its discovered fount:
restored, engraved, the polished, oiled stone
renewed by seminary hands–
the water mirroring

those woven shadows of a forward spring
where ice, last month, had smothered roots
and shrouded ecstasy
beneath our blizzard's drifts. Around the room
mosaics bear medieval names
I cannot explicate

or even recognize. Icons create
archaic circles, as if bone
and blood, once cold, could mount
and recombine, until a body stands
within this room, its cabinets shut
and locked after each Mass.

Mendelssohn

*~Elijah: An Oratorio with Words
from the Old Testament (Op. 70, 1846)*

I'll always carry matches with me now.
Though I'm no priest of forests or of hills
they have my sympathies, they don't deserve
to have their sacrifices overlooked
or burnt by unseen hands disparaging
their loves, their passions or their revelries.

The chorus, in angelic black, descends
into the pews, the walls are stucco white
and hold unfigured crucifixes, bare
of any suffering, but voices call
in harmony for every Baalist priest
to be cut down, by swords, beside the stream.

And so, with all of us, by stone or flame,
or sharpened gleaming edges flashing down
in choruses of mockery revered
only by gathered ravens, who would feast.
No benefit of orchestra or voice
could reclaim what our ecstasy reserved.

Our act is over. Near the sacristy
the singers gather in their chaos, flutes
and cymbals passing near us without sound
as unfamiliar exultations weave
black robes together, threatening the wind
with wingbeats sharpened on Elijah's gold.

Grace

The porch, unpainted, falls to disrepair
peacocks contend the fences, and her swans
contest each scattered kernel, flung to ground
as if by unseen hands. All undeserved
benevolence is evident in one
sunlit display, between the half-designed

or accidental blossomings of limbs
moving by days from red through pink to white
almost immune from frost, as her long spring
escapes whatever winds are still to come.
And yet, her garden, and her landscape bears
tormented lacerations. In these scars

reflected in her form, we understand
the wounds we suffer open us to grace,
as if the violence is a gift, as if
the slashing blade or pointed horn could rend
more than our flesh, could open us to earth
and strengthen us to bear that charity

we never thought could make us whole. Those birds
continue their displays in sunlight as
the petals fall around them, as if snow
were coming out of season, and could freeze
our words before we understood, or keep
those wings from beating past the broken fence.

Evanescence

Old Polynesians fabricated guards
of fronds for graves, backdropped with tapa cloth,
the whole scene like an altar, then they left
the elements to do their silent work
and as the forms reverted back to dust
so did their memories of those they'd lost.

But we desire permanence, and set
our works, for preservation, into leaves.
I've watched the saffron monks designing forms
throat-singing their geometry. The sand
is, really, fine crushed quartz, dyed to their needs,
the figured symmetries are all received

and after weeks of prayerful work, they sweep
in rituals the sand into a vase
and bear it off to streambanks, rivers, shores:
it only matters that the water flows.
They empty out what had been beautiful
reminding them and us that all is lost,

our thoughts of permanence are vanity.
I think of Li-Po, folding into boats
the graceful lines of slow calligraphy
and launching them onto the mountain stream
watching their progress till they lose their form
or vanish over quiet waterfalls.

Lied du Chêne

The small oaks of the maquis countryside
are not the verdant trees you, growing, knew.
Those seem invisible. Their pointed leaves
whose green was never ours, unite the day
with evening through dusk. Each man believes
his are the limbs of paradise, while blue
reflections cast a luminescence near

the outlines of each branch. It may appear
as halo or as crown, almost as smoke
above each bough if you look close enough.
Its sign is sanctuary. You may pray
to unseen veiled gods, but oak is rough
and tangible. Its cover becomes cloak
in which a group of men may hide their trace,

where passages are masked. A hidden face
confirms our reveries, and we create
out of these sprigs of lavender and vines
exquisite vintages. Our disarray
confirms the unique character of wines
produced among these hills. It is our fate
that we become the earth, just as we burn

the winter's growth, whose tongues of fire turn
like constellations, round across this sky
where red Sirocco dust transforms the air
even in darkness. Red, the subtle way
a woman moves along a path, her hair
lit only by those stars whose songs imply
those oaks were left as signpost. Signal. Guide.

Amber

Rough congealations of the frozen sea,
polished with tripoli or ash
from jewelers' cigarettes,
may bear inclusions of primeval days:
intact mantids or dragonflies
preserved as if their wings

if gently freed, could fly. If coverings
could be dissolved, perhaps they might
renew their ardor here.
But no. We drill the golden ornament
and interbraid the champagne light
until their curve suggests

a pendant lost between her veiled breasts,
a gift to hide, or briefly flash
in quickly angled eyes
or warm against her skin as she forgets
the almost whispered blandishment
she thought she'd still recall

after his hands lifted her pashmine shawl,
but in her mind, the stones appear
to crystallize sublime
cycles of ecstasy, and in her gaze
the captured ardor of this time
becomes her memory.

Yungas Valley

No man should have to risk his life for leaves.
But if you farmed those slopes would you descend
four hundred meters to the valley floor
then crossing rapids to the other shore
climb back to the same height? The time you'd spend
could be employed in tending to your crop.

And so you'd string your lines, facing the drop
with pulleys and with cables, galvanized
against the mountain climate and drawn tight
from one bank to the other with a slight
slack curve to slow you down. It's all devised
from scavenged gear. Those bolts are held with thread

and harnesses are simply torn cloth, spread
into a sling, and tied. There are no brakes:
just take some leaves and hold them to the line
to check your speed. The cable's soft incline
leaves little space for slips. Careless mistakes
mean plunging to the rapids. Just last year

a woman's husband fell. It's still unclear
exactly how it happened. Did he tie
his harness overtight? No-one can know.
And yet, if you look up, you'll see the slow
progress of a lone man across this sky
flying towards the vision he believes.

Rutter's Requiem

I can remember other concerts played
in sacred spaces, where the choir stood
on escalated benches whose long wings
hovered above the orchestra's drawn strings,
above arranged trumpets. The olivewood
cross bore no body then, so Latin lines

seemed out of place. The mysteries of signs
were absent from the walls. All I could do
was watch the lips of singers. Altos held
their phrases half a breath, hoping to meld
their sound with woodwinds, straight-toned, on beat, true.
It's not what I prefer. I want to lust

after the beautiful soprano's hushed
vibrato tessitura, wish her gown
might fall away, leaving only those pearls
against her breathing skin, melodic swirls
guiding my steps outside, leading me down
into the forest's labyrinth, where leaves

fall at her will. But here, each bowed head grieves,
and we will go on grieving while the songs
continue, as these harmonies of breath
surround with grace even this present death,
redeeming my iniquities, our wrongs,
a moment, until blended voices fade.

VII
ECHOES

"Love made them meet in a well-ordered dance."
~Sir John Davies

Edward Robert Hughes (1851-1914).
Midsummer Eve, 1908.

Folklife Festival

The Mall in Washington: extended green
of well-planned lawns, the brown of gravel walks
burning beneath a summer sun, no clouds
to break the heat. And here, imported jeeps
perform as in Columbia, while crowds
look on, half-interested. A woman talks
in amplified excitement of the moves

accomplished drivers turn. The crowd approves
then saunters to pavilions and the shade.
There, at each booth, a different show: how one
taught herself carving, how another reaps,
with just a blade, bamboo. The cutting done,
he dries the cane three weeks. Its peacock jade
turns brown before he trims it down to length

and builds pavilions with it, whose dried strength
is code compliant, even here. Beneath
the shade of one, a man turns ivory
on homemade lathes, and as he works, he keeps
almost silent. A woman translates. She
holds back from telling how the palmnut sheath
is cut away from dried fruit to reveal

what seems white wood or tusk. Her words conceal
anxiety of speaking for the man
who, in his country, is revered for art
made of the simplest things. Praises she heaps
in words he cannot understand impart
a comprehension each onlooker can
take home from this weekend's constructed scene.

A Tail Full of Suns

Green gold and blue, the Whistler, stylized
and now enclosed within another room
was only painted. Meant for porcelain
it seemed the fruit of argument and loss
although some butterflies still hide along
the gilded edges of a woman's frame.

But I remember sunlight, and the trees
that dappled afternoons above the long
processions of the young. In following
we turned a corner of the path and found
a panoramic incandescent blue
more brilliant than our young imaginings.

Of course, we read it as the universe
laid bare in sacrifice, as if the grace
of beauty could return and be our lives,
as if it turned to face us, while the sun
still slanted from the west, still warmed the ground
and lit chaotic wings above the eyes.

But better, now, to think of cedar posts
with one bird perched on each, or think of gates
with seven on a rail in the shade
now that each gate around us has been bent
diagonal by beauty's weight, and latched
enclosing us as if in painted rooms.

Double Vision

Balloon or bird above the waving trees,
maybe a kite unstrung, perhaps
a single twist of smoke?
These eyes begin to blur all distant things:
steeples against uncluttered sky,
even the moon succumbs

and cannot hold itself as one, becomes
a diagram with intersects
stark white, where unison
converging crescent faces intertwine
themselves, while floating in and out
of focus as I gaze.

Each time is different. There are some days
when I'm convinced my sight collects
specific contoured wings
enough to help me name, identify
or recollect, lets me refine
the earth into its parts

but always, as I watch, the image starts
to separate, comparison
escapes, and wings collapse
like broken kites, above the swaying oak
I can't distinguish now without
my doubled expertise.

Photograph

She's looking at me as she looks away
the glass reflects her image, and reflects
its own, reversed. Her pearls mirroring
themselves mirror red lipstick and her skin
remaking prisms reinvoked in light
captured behind her autofocused lens.

Here, endlessly repeated we become
something beyond ourselves, between the two
laced images, there must be light, unseen
but real, so the glass can duplicate
appearances we cannot intercept
without its aid. Lacking the silvering

we could not guess what empty air contains
or reconstruct impressions of ourselves.
And so we carefully apply argent
until technique becomes invisible
since brushstrokes cloud reflections and become
persistent careless flaws each time we gaze.

She's taught me this: describing images
is mere obsession, we must look between
the doubled panes of glass: there, empty space
is filled with unimagined reckonings
and if we train ourselves to see them we
may yet discover something more than light.

Tatu

Our cashier bore a tattoo on his arm.
At first, I thought a pattern, then I saw
it looked like flowered verse. I praised fine work
and asked him of its origins, and why
he thought to wear a song. Shocked, he replied
the work was read out at her funeral.

This art involves the dermis. Needles plunge
a thousand times a minute halfway through
live skin, and inject ink. Homogenized
and damaged layers hold the pigment still
until new granulated tissue forms,
and dyes are stabilized in fibroblasts.

A mummy from the fifth millennium
had tattooed skin. In Laos, ink was used
as shield, or as armament against
unknown malevolence. Young women wore
irezumi to beckon or to charm,
or consecrated arms to goddesses.

Our young man chose the meaning of his verse
and held still as the needle pierced raw skin,
as blood was wiped away. Now, as I write
I think of him, his pain, the permanence,
and hope to make each word worthy of all
the suffering he bore as memory.

Fisher

Clear sky past dawn, rose granite peaks, moraine
tumbling along their faces, newly lit
by sunlight not yet settled on the red
veined leaves of sugar maples. Shadows spread
across the streambank where forked swallows flit,
catching the early swarming gnats who lift

themselves above the stream. A few leaves drift
along the current, swirling near a rock
on which a lone man, dressed against the cold,
prepares himself. His supple fingers hold
straight sections of split cane. They interlock
to make the flyrod whole. Twelve yards of line

move in an S-curve through chill air. The fine
leader conveys a fly. The loop unfurls
and, laid out straight before him, slowly falls
across the water. Now his hand recalls
the line, and lays it back. An eddy swirls,
a rainbow rising from the water takes

the unbarbed fly. His twisting motion makes
the hand, almost by instinct, lightly flick
the rodtip, just as sunstreak rays descend
onto the cutbank trees, whose colors blend
with rose-quartz veins, late aspens, and the quick
curved wings of swallows lighting this terrain.

Cloud Ladders

An egg has feathers, and a chestnut horse
is not a horse. If you are light, refrain
from glowing: all the beauty you possess
may blind neighbors. A journey yesterday
begins tomorrow. If you could undress
you'd disappear, or I would, and the rain
would fall on both of us in drops but flow

as streams towards our feet until they slow
and form a single pool where we might stand
connected. While linked rings can be unbound,
both sky and earth combine to make a day.
A turning wheel does not touch the ground.
Five elements are fingers on a hand
working together, but my framing square

is angled by degrees, and so no chair
I've ever made conforms to heaven's straight
design. And so with long grained perfect trees:
sheer trunks are cut, bent ones allowed to stay
and grow. The bird, arriving, quickly flees
when greeted by well-wishers at the gate.
Lily and Rose are loveliness, but deer

would run from their approach. Beneath the clear
stream's surface, near the bridge they're crossing, fish,
minnows perhaps, small silver things, cavort
but can we know they're happy? Can we say
we know their minds, or ours? Do we consort
with their same joy, or is it our one wish
to simply understand the river's source?

Cymatics

Does sound have form? And can we illustrate
through talcum patterns on a iron square
elucidated correspondences
between the visual and what we hear?
Or are there undiscovered harmonies
between the audible and crystalline?

Suspend a tempered steel plate from strings
or mount it on a single columned stand
and dust the flattened surface with ground salt.
Then draw a rosined bow across its edge
with one quick stroke, as if the violin
were only resonate to one swift note.

Now watch: the chaos of excited grains
will change to mandalas in monochrome
and represent acoustic energy
made visual: harmonics of the sand
which demonstrate the patterned unity
connecting all experience, our words

made physical, embodied in this dust,
articulating resonance between
the sound designed to create ecstasy
in any who would hear and unseen forms
working within us as we reflect sounds
that resonate with everything we've known.

Resurrection Fern

Just outside Mobile Bay, a thunderstorm
confused the branches as I ran inside
and rifled every limb in my small wood.
That evening, I walked the littered ground
and there, among the uncombed Spanish moss
and camphor limbs contorted by the wind

I found an oak bough, broken as it held
unbending to the onshore rush, it's bark
encircled by a resurrection fern
along it's whole length, six full feet or more
and dragged it back up to the garden gate.
I cut it down a bit, so it would span

with little overhang the rough uprights
that marked the path's transition from the coarse
ungoverned forest to the laid out beds
of efflorescent tropicals whose roots
could never bear acidic sand without
the cultivations of my careful hands.

It held there all my time along that bay
dying each afternoon, the curling brown
of dried fronds pointing to the daily clouds
and our late rain returning them to green
thus promising the gardens might return
after each thunderstorm, and bloom again.

Compline

In ringing midnight, bells are not consumed
but lamps must be refilled, candles replaced,
even the pages of these books grow old,
their letters miracles of red and gold.
One leaf shows where some ancient finger traced
a final chant of evening, which we

sing in remembrance of the mystery.
How is it, then, when burning with this same
intensity, in this transforming flare,
that we are undiminished? Well aware
both of the light around us and the flame
within our breath, we still feel restored,

as if we were a vessel which had poured
all substance out and been replenished, fresh
with burning waters flowing through us now,
and grateful for their presence, we allow
the stream to flow through veins, replace our flesh
with light and songs of praise grown crystalline,

and when the songs are finished, we begin
to withdraw quietly, to contemplate
this mystery of darkness and this light
illuminating every step of night,
and closing all our windows, we await
transfigurement, like roses which have bloomed.

Departure

Within this circle her embellished hand
lights candles, and the incense starts to burn
as my voice calls to any who may hear
for peace: this flame, our smoke, and sound converge
in supplicating vortexes across
the empty space between us filled with light

and as a fire, burning kindled brands
renews the transformations of a time
when figures danced around a central blaze
while others harmonized devotions to
the winds that bore their branching flames towards
a sky as luminous as any song

or as a couple, in a central square
with interlacing hands, transform the earth
by leaping through the changing, burning winds
that swirl around the patterned wood conveyed
by children singing preparations for
a summers night's abundant harvesting

so we, in that small room, imagined tongues
of peaceful flame from candles purified
by our two whispered voices, and the air
though quiet, filled with unexplained replies
harmonious and delicate, transformed
a moment, in the space between our hands.

The Dark Wood

I wanted to write paradise. I would
create, with words, a space where each may dwell
who comes to read. A quiet song, small words
almost as calming as the wind, light birds
their feathers shadow-flashing, or the swell
breaking into a wave across the sand.

But how can I, who must contend, withstand
the vanity of anger, find release
from constant striving, imitate a saint
or gold friend, limit sailing, find restraint
unbound, as if those wings knew only peace,
or only knew the tiled fountain walls

only the coppiced branch, whose fork recalls
the skill of gardeners I don't possess?
Their sharpened blades can form a boundary hedge
or perfect angles, pyramids, a wedge
pointing towards a spring the long flights bless
since water is our gift. The hovering

voices behind those trees find room to sing
whenever I can still myself, renounce
the arguments of vanity I hold
so close, always, within. If I enfold
those wings and voices, I may yet pronounce
the paradise I sensed within that wood.

Incarnant Sounds

I stop. For now it's finished. All around
there's something moving through the air, as if
the very breeze is filled with creatures from
some other place. I've never known these sounds
to grow incarnate, swirling through bent light
of any spring, late afternoon or dusk

I cannot tell. I've heard the stories. Some
have felt these things as music, some as wind
and some as words they cannot comprehend.
And one, two dozen years ago, lay still
while all around her danced malevolent
but unnamed spirits? Who can say? But she

felt something in the eddys that surround
us always, most unnoticed days, and marked
intent. Then she cried out, and suddenly
she was delivered. For myself, I heard
no music, saw no dancing, only felt
a whirling energy, an animate

confusion of spun luminescence and
wanted to stand and flee at once. Instead
I called to her, and took her in my arms
shaken and mute with inexpressible
unbounded cadences, and held her as
our Autumn light retreated into dusk.

Epilogue

I made my love a garden of these songs:
the only place where lotus coincides
with mandeville– a harmony of rose
all perfumed to her choice, and though her eyes
almost could see wisteria entwined
with purple clematis. A cardinal's nest

was indication of intended birds:
swallows and golden pheasants intermixed
while merlins winged their cruciforms above
the adjured peacocks milling everywhere:
feathers and sunlight, mottled koi, and wind
creating winding ripples through the reeds.

Mirrors and follies magnified delight
invoking inland seas and hovered skies.
The swirling breeze seemed to arrive at will
while feather grasses swayed, even bamboo,
though veiled by thunbergia, would dance.
Chromatic harmonies seemed all the scene

required for completion. Who could say
eventuals in such a place would be
delimited, or unreality
would overwhelm this comprehension? Love,
permit me voyage only through your will
since all my charms are overthrown within.

Wind

I would unlearn this gift, and make a song
worthy of you, beyond the boundaries of
these constant footsteps, racing to a goal
a few lines on. The resonance I've learned
is not the wind around us. If I could
I'd let the harmonies I labor go

and simply draw your figure on the air
between us, as if form and words were one.
Take then these hands, my love, that tap the wood
ten times per line, take all the sounds I know
all the devices I have ever used
to beckon charm delight or mesmerize,

consume them in your vortex, where all things
are one: I give them to you freely. Let
their energy be yours. They're all I have
of grace, these distillations of the breath
of all who walked this earth before, and sang
their love or loss, or simply what they saw–

allow their song, through mine, to feed you, love,
then sing! It is your gift, the breathing voice
that lets me breathe again as you return
all I have given you, now changed to wind
moving around us, as the sound of bells
recalls us to this peaceful moment here.

Glossary

This glossary of words, names and terms is added by the author for the convenience of readers to enhance their enjoyment and access to the full range of language and meaning as used in the poems. The briefest definition or explanation is provided only to support the meaning in the poem.

Accoutrements:– Small items related to one's practice or craft. Miranda prefers pearls and cashmere, but is not above resorting to gold bangles. She eschews ankle bracelets.

Adjured:– Sworn or promised. Spoken of truthfully. Said of something that has been written about honestly.

Adornments:– Various ornaments designed to enhance the appearance of the wearer. Here, often a metonymy: the beauty of Miranda's wrought pins is metaphor for her own.

Afterimage:– Some scenes are so luminescent they remain with us, even after we close our eyes.

Alabaster:– See under Pound, Ezra:
"The 'age demanded' chiefly a mould in plaster,
Made with no loss of time,
A prose kinema, not, not assuredly, alabaster
Or the "sculpture" of rhyme."

Alto:– A voice range of beautiful singers, high, but below the range of a Soprano. Never say that to an Alto.

Ambuscade:– A peaceful ambush. See under Ovid:
"Just the sort of light, with curtains drawn
wherein to lay inviting ambuscade."

Anachie Gordon:– An ancient British folksong, possibly with Swedish roots. A sad love song in which the two main characters perish. Also, the first song I ever heard Miranda sing.

Anacostia:– A river in Maryland which debouches into the Chesapeake. The Northwest Branch flows behind our home. I can see it from my office window.

Anteros:– Brother of Eros. He's way cooler than his sibling.

Aphrodite:– The mother of Anteros. Also, the descendant of Inanna.

Argent:– Tincture of silver, sometimes used of silver itself, sometimes called white silver.

Artifice:– This word should be read here with positive connotations. A "small A" word for the devices of Art.

Assonance:– A sound trick of poets which I strive to avoid. Any appearance here is purely accidental, an unpreventable statistical anomaly.

Asymmetric:– Slightly off form, out of round, unbalanced.

Auguries:– Omens, sayings, interpretations of signs, predictions of the future. See under Blake: "uguries of Innocence:"
> "To see a world in a grain of sand
> And a heaven in a wild flower,
> Hold infinity in the palm of your hand
> And eternity in an hour."

Azure:– The Southeast coast of France from somewhere near Hyères all the way to Menton is often called the Côte d'Azur because of the incredible blueness of the water at certain times of year.

Baalist:– Local priests of the predominant religion in the Eastern Mediterranean circa 1000 BCE.

Baird:– Number four son. Also, a Scottish word for poet.

Balustrades:– An architectural term, referring to the small posts that support marble stair railings. Each may be crafted like a good line of verse.

Bandsaw:– Woodworking machine with a continuous bladed saw strung around two opposing wheels (end on end) and used to roughly cut wood. The "Grizzly" in my shop has two fourteen inch wheels.

Basilica:– A term of art for a certain type of church, usually large. Definitions vary. The one mentioned here is also called The National Shrine, a domed structure in Washington, D.C.

Beatitude:– Any of the concise declarations meant to be taken as articles of faith in several religions. Also, a form of well-being characterized by intense joy.

Belladonna:– Literally, beautiful lady. Also, a poisonous plant of the Nightshade family, like tobacco or the tomato, whose sap, when distilled and applied topically, enlarges the pupils.

Belle:– French descriptive term for a beautiful woman: 'There she is, *La Belle*.'

Blandishment:– A flattering compliment meant to caress the spirit and coax a gentle response.

Boethius:– Sixth Century writer famous for his devotion to Lady Philosophy. Invented the Wheel of Fortune. Favorite philosopher of Chaucer.

Bordeaux:– A region of Southwestern France known for delectable wines and women of exceptional beauty.

Bowl gouge:– A hardened steel tool used to shape interior forms on a wood lathe.

Brocades:– Any of a number of shuttle-woven fabrics, often intricate and incorporating golden thread.

Brushhooks:– A long-handled hooked machete meant to clear wild land. Requires an extremely careful swing.

Burin:– A hand tool used in intaglio engraving, most often to scratch a line in a copper plate. If sharp enough, it often leaves a telltale burr.

Camphor:– A large evergreen tree of the Laurel family, native to Southern China. Naturalized along the Gulf Coast. Extremely fragrant.

***Carmina Burana*:**– A set of 13th Century Latin poems of unknown authorship, set to music in 1936 by Orff. You've heard "O! Fortuna" countless times. It was the featured piece at the first concert Miranda and I attended together.

Carmine:– A deep red dye derived from the crushed bodies of scale insects. Early uses included paint and stained glass. One of the jewel tones.

Catalpa:– A large white flowered tree typical of the Eastern forests of North America. Around our Beltway, they grow like weeds.

Cellar (door):– Often cited by linguists and poets as the most beautiful set of sounds in the English language. I'm pretty sure they're pulling our leg.

Censer:– Any of a number of devices used for burning incense, from elaborate metal vessels to simple strips of wood. I find them scattered all over the house, and even in my shop.

Chanticleer:– A character in Chaucer who comes to a sad end. Also, an all-male ensemble of *a capella* singers, beloved of Miranda. Look for their version of Biebl's "Ave Maria."

Chêne:– A particular kind of oak tree associated with the woods and thickets of provincial France.

Chignon:– A hairstyle popular in ancient Greece and early China. A decorative pin was used to keep the hair in place. The removal of the pin sometimes suggests exquisite drama.

Chromatic:– A musical scale characterized by twelve pitches, each a semitone apart. Popular with Medieval composers. In China, the same scale was known as Shí-èr-lü, in India, Sargam.

Clematis:– A popular large flowered climbing vine. Its name is often mispronounced.

Coloratura:– A rare and exquisite operatic voice type, characterized by agile runs and leaps, light, and quick as a songbird's. Miranda is a lyric coloratura soprano.

Columbina:– Literally, a small dove. Often used for a character in light opera and Commedia dell'Arte: a beautiful young woman, desired by the lead role.

Compline:– The final set of prayers in the Litany of Hours. Also used for night prayer, or the beginning of the Great Silence.

Conjure:– A means of summoning something outside daily experience, by voice or gesture. The elaborate movements of Miranda's hands often presage the arrival of something new. I was amazed to find similar movements depicted in both late and early works of art. For an example, see Leighton's "Invocation."

Consanguinate:– Relationship by blood or common ancestor. See Crane's:
"Infinite consanguinity it bears—
This tendered theme of you that light
Retrieves from sea plains where the sky
Resigns a breast that every wave enthrones;"

Copperheads:– The most prevalent variety of poisonous snake in Washington, DC. I look for them every time I walk through our forest.

Coppiced:– A tree, or branch of a tree, which has been trimmed to take advantage of its growth habit. Many urban trees are coppiced in Europe.

Corniched:– The Grand Corniche is a curving road following the upper route between Nice and Monte Carlo. A house built along the same ridges is said to be "corniched."

Crandall:– A stonemasons tool, resembling a hammer, used for dressing rough blocks of stone.

Crosscut:– A method of cutting any kind of stock, from wood to marble, across its axis.

Crozet:– A small town in central Virginia, close to the Blue Ridge. There's a small Trappistine abbey in the hills, not marked on any maps, where a fine Gouda is sold.

Cruciform:– A term describing the shape of falcons and kestrels hovering on the wind.

Cymatics:– The study of tangible sound, or of materials moved and patterned by sound.

Daphne:– A laurel tree. Also, a woman pursued by Apollo, god of poetry, who escaped the poet by being transformed into a laurel. A laurel wreath became the traditional mark of poets. See Pound, Ezra: "I ask for a wreath that will not crush my head."

Distaff:– Anything normally associated with feminine skills. Originally, a tool used in conjunction with a spinning wheel, a way to hold wool or flax before it moves onto the spindle.

Earthsigns:– Elements of a system, now seldom practiced, of predicting the future by observing variances in natural phenomena. Not to be confused with astrological groupings.

Efflorescent:– The state or moment of the most profuse flowering, the primary goal of cultivation.

***Elijah*:–** Felix Mendelssohn's most widely performed oratorio. The story is surprisingly violent.

Enchantment:– A sequence of chanted words intended to bring about the fulfillment of a desire on the part of the speaker. Can be whispered, or even repeated silently. In Miranda's case, even these may be sublimated into a simple physical wish.

Enthralled:– Held in thrall, fascinated, literally bound by a cast spell. See under Keats, but with mercy.

Eros:– Son of Aphrodite, brother of Anteros. Falls in love with Psyche, who was also known as "butterfly," which happens to be the nickname Miranda's vocal mentor gave her in reference to her light, agile voice, which flits beautifully from note to note.

Ferdinand:– A minor character in *The Tempest*. He falls madly in love with Miranda, on sight.

Fibroblast:– Medical term for connective tissues beneath the skin. I'm not that kind of doctor.

Flax:– The gift of Frigga, used in the production of linen.

Flow:– Term used by Mihály Csíkszentmihályi to describe the state of artistic production, or frame of mind of the artist during the creative act. Characterized by an intense focus, channeled emotion, and energized immersion so profound time and even the goal of the act cease to be perceived.

Follies:– Architectural structures in European landscape gardens, often erected to suggest vistas of ancient ruins.

Fortuna, Dame:– Goddess of fortune, both good and bad. Augustine railed against her, Boethius embraced her. She spins the wheel.

Framboise:– Starred French chefs often place a bit of raspberry or melon in high end Champagne. At first, I was surprised, just as I was surprised at being served warm beer in London. Thankfully, I refrained from asking for ice.

Gazelle:– Descriptive term for Miranda's light, agile leaps when walking. Also, a poetic form beloved of Lorca.

Glissade:– The process of descending glaciers while wearing hiking boots. Also, a move in classical ballet, and a fencing technique for disarming opponents.

Gloss:– Brief marginal notation of a literary text. An extended gloss is sometimes called a pony.

Grout:– Decorative construction material for sealing the joints between tiles. When I used porcelain white, Miranda objected, and had me replace it with ivory.

Indigo:– Dye originally derived from crushed leaves of woad, later from plants native to India. One of my favorite colors. Miranda has several scarves in various shades, but inclines to purple herself.

Inflected:– See under Stevens:
"I do not know which to prefer,
The beauty of inflections
Or the beauty of innuendoes,
The blackbird whistling
Or just after."

Interlace:– One of the primary metaphors in all my thoughts of Miranda. It first occurred to me at a Chanticleer concert, as I listened to the voices weave themselves together. See also "The Interlace Structure of Beowulf." (Leyerle, Toronto: 1967)

Irezumi:– Japanese form of tattooing.

Ivushka:– Russian folksong. The lyrics concern a willow tree. When sung by Miranda, it would melt even the stoniest of hearts. She learned it while singing with Slavic Mosaic.

James:– Our youngest son, named after his uncle. Also, after the pragmatic philosopher, William James, who said, "Nature in her unfathomable designs has mixed us of clay and flame, of brain and mind. The two things hang indubitably together and determine each other's being. But how or why, no mortal may ever know."

Jewelweed:– Impatiens-like plant, native to Eastern North America. Its juice is said to be effective against poison ivy reactions. Often found growing near stands of poison ivy. Should be applied immediately to affected areas.

Jouissance:– French for joy, or a joyful state. Colloquially, a discrete term for *croissance* or climax. Before Lacan, almost always feminine. Jacques should have paid more attention to his grammar lessons.

Kohl:– Cosmetic used for darkening the area around the eyes. In ancient times, it contained lead. Most modern kohls are made from charcoal.

Koi:– Japanese carp, actually native to China. Butterfly koi have long, graceful fins. Garden ponds are incomplete without them.

Lacrymosa:– Part of the "Dies Irae" sequence in the *Requiem Mass*. See under Mozart. Also, if you prefer, Regina Spektor.

Lalique:– *Fin de siècle* French glassmaker, known for vases and jewelry. Miranda has several brooches and pins styled after Lalique.

Lapis:– Semi-precious stone, often blue with gold inclusions. Famously celebrated by Yeats.

Lath:– Strips of wood (often redwood) used in construction of shade houses for sensitive plants. Also, shorthand for *Look at the Harlequins*.

Lathe:– A powered machine tool intended for turning wooden objects. Mine has a seven inch swing, which means it can turn a fourteen inch wide bowl. Can also be used to form spindles for furniture making.

Lavender:– Miranda's favorite scent. Grows best in dry climates, like Alta California or Grasse. Here, it tends to drown in the rain and humidity.

Lied:– An art song, in German mainly from the 19th Century. Most poems set to music qualify as Lieder. Miranda introduced me to Faure's .

Li-Po (Li Bai):– Chinese poet, fond of wine. One of the "eight immortals of the wine cup." Liked to fold his poems into little boats and let them float away on the stream. Some say he drowned trying to drunkenly embrace the moon's reflection in the Yangtze River.

Locust:– Here, not an insect, but a tree. There's a bowl on Miranda's nightstand turned from a Black Locust felled by an ice storm.

Luaun:– Generic term for decorative plywood made from renewable tropical trees.

Lunations:– Crescents or whole-rounds in mosaic or tile suggesting various stages of the moon.

Mandalas:– Decorative Sanskrit circles, often composed using colored sands. Rose windows are their cognates in the West. Rarely, a descriptive term used in discussions of certain formal poems.

Mandeville:– Flowering vine, sometimes considered hallucinogenic, and, rarely, employed as aphrodisiac. Also, a 17th Century writer known for his "Fable of the Bees."

Merlin:– A small species of circumpolar falcon. Winters in temperate climates. Medieval texts describe it as the ideal "falcon for a lady."

Mirabai:– Medieval Indian mystical dancer and poet. Lover of Krishna. Some disapproved of her habit of dancing from village to village, called her immodest, and tried to poison her. Many of the poems she composed survive.

Miranda:– A miraculous being, whose existence could be neither imagined nor predicted, who insists she's "just a mortal woman." A protean changeling, whose transformations, if revealed, would mystify the most jaded skeptic. The center of a whirlwind. A coloratura soprano. Also, by the grace of providence, my wife.

Mitered:– A means of deftly cutting wood joints at an angle. Since they are often used in conjunction with other miters, each angle must be perfect or the error is magnified.

Mobile:– A small city in coastal Alabama. If you're there, move. If you're not there, don't go. I went. I was lucky to escape with my life.

Möbius:– Nineteenth Century mathematician who invented a twisted "non-orientable two-dimensional surface with only one side when embedded in three-dimensional Euclidean space." Yikes! Suffice it to say an ant could walk around all of its edges and return to his starting point without crossing his own path.

Mockingbird:– My favorite bird in California. It can repeat any song it hears once. They were more common here in Jefferson's age. It's said he kept one in his office at all times, even as president.

Moraine:– A collection of rocks and debris pushed in front of a glacier, or left behind after the glacier melts. Sometimes included very large boulders.

Nightingales:– I'm told these birds exist. I've never seen one, nor ever heard its song.

Oak:– A coarse-grained, rough-textured wood, hard and difficult to work with for furniture making. I ran some through my planer and nearly ruined the knives. Since then, I've stuck to cherry and maple.

Ocotillos:– Hardy plants native to the Borrego desert. For most of the year, they look like dried eight foot octopi. In winter, their green stems are tipped with red flowers.

Oleanders:– Flowering shrubs with poisonous, milky sap. They do well in the desert, but can't stand Eastern winters.

Olivewood:– The preferred wood for traditional rosaries. Takes on a rich luster after much handling. Some say the best olivewood comes from the slopes of Mount Carmel. Miranda has several such olivewood rosaries.

Ovid:– Nearly sacred poet of *The Art of Love*. Devoted to Corinna. She's sometimes unpleasant to him. I'm told he wrote some other poems, as well. Things ended poorly for him.

Palmnut:– South American source of vegetable ivory. Can be carved, and even shaped on a lathe, often into jewelry.

Panis Angelicus:– a Communion hymn written by Aquinas and set recently by César Franck.

Pashmine:– Soft colorful fabric woven from the fine wool of Himalayan goats. The goats, known as Changthangi, can survive temperatures as low as minus twenty degrees centigrade without shelter.

Passionate Virtuosity:– A term first seen in John Barth's *Chimera*: "Making love and telling stories both take more than good technique—but it's only the technique that we can talk about. Heartfelt ineptitude has its appeal, so does heartless skill. But what you want is passionate virtuosity."

Peacock:– Miranda's totem bird. There is a picture of one in nearly every room.

Pearl:– My favorite poem from medieval English times. Often attributed to the "Gawain" poet. It has as many layers as the gem itself.

Peregrine:– Literally, pilgrim. Here, one of the larger falcons. They nest in the Basilica every year.

Pheasant:– Beautiful prairie bird which should never be shotgunned. A Golden Pheasant often visited my garden in Western Pennsylvania.

Plinth:– The square stone at the base of an architectural column. Jude the Obscure famously perches on one.

Plumeria:– A tropical flowering shrubby tree native to New Zealand and South America. Fragrant, but difficult to grow in temperate climates.

Plywood:– Believe it or not, this, along with MDF, is considered a better substrate for veneer than hardwood.

Promenade:– A wide pathway near the Mediterranean shore in the French city of Nice. Called *d'Anglais* because only the English tourists thought it healthy to walk in the sun. The locals considered them crazy.

Prosody:– The study of poetic technique. Much of it has more to do with linguistics than poetry.

Proteus:– Ancient god who could change forms at will, and knew many secrets. If you could just hold on through the transformations, you could discover many mysteries.

Quotidian:– French for Daily. Widely naturalized into English.

Rapier:– A thin, long, sharp-pointed sword, usually with a bladeguard. James imagines them ideally suited for fending off dinosaurs.

Rasa:– Indian term concerning the nature of Art. Originally, there were eight rasas, with corresponding colors and gods. Love songs were presided over by Vishnu, and suggested light green. Around the 6th Century, a ninth rasa was added.

Rattlesnake:– The only American monster. I once killed a twelve-footer as it coiled next to Julian's outdoor crib. With the six month old Julian inside. I have no regrets.

Redwood:– I grew up seeing giant Sequoias trees fairly frequently. In my mind's eye, I thought all trees were supposed to be that big.

Resnake:– The process of rethreading electrical cable through pre-existing openings in structural beams. See under Romex.

Retted:– See also retter, retting. A process of submerging harvested flax stems in a handy nearby pond or bog. It takes about two weeks, and allows the fibers to be more easily separated before being drawn out on the spinning wheel.

Reveals:– An exposed section of a window, door, or furniture frame. Often includes miters at the corners.

Revery:– A transcendent, dreamlike state, easily induced by a simple glance at Miranda's form.

Rhyme:– Here, not a sonic device, but a structural element. Many say rhyme was invented in China, travelled along the Silk Road, through Persia and Arabia, and arrived in Europe, through Moorish Spain, sometime around the 10th Century. In any case, it was unknown to Homer, Virgil, and the poet of *Beowulf*.

Rockville:– A quotidian city in Maryland, just outside the Capital Beltway. Main claim to fame: F. Scott Fitzgerald is buried there, beside Zelda. Site of many early coffees with Miranda, and one notable lunch.

Romex:– Electrical cable used for indoor wiring. For most applications, select twelve-two with ground. Always buy it by the box: you need way more than you think.

Routing:– The process of forming or shaping wood molding or trim on a router table. My Precision Router Lift was a gift from Miranda. I made the router table to go with it.

Rubythroats:– The only species of Hummingbird found in Eastern North America. California has more than a dozen species.

Rune:– Element of an ancient system of "whisper" writing. In Finnish, "runot" is the word for song. Sometimes associated with incantations. Displaced by the Latin alphabet c. 1000 CE.

Rushlights:– A medieval candle or small torch, made by soaking bound stems of rushes (hardy waterside and bog plants) with flammable liquid. Prevalent in the countryside until the 19th Century.

Rutter:– Twentieth Century British composer. You've heard his *Requiem* a hundred times without knowing it.

Sacristy:– A semi-sacred room wherein ritual vestments and furnishings are stored.

Serenity:– Film based on my favorite American programme, cancelled after a single season. Most memorable character: Inara Serra. Also, a state of contemplation.

Shards:– One of the most overused terms in contemporary poetry. I'm shocked to find it here. At least it's only once.

Short grain:– Term of wood working art describing pieces cut across the grain. Long grain pieces are cut along, or with, the grain.

Silvering:– The coating which changes panes of glass into mirrors. Originally actual silver, most is now made from aluminum.

Sirocco:– A hot, Southerly wind which blows the red dust of the Sahara all the way to the Southern Coast of France, sometimes reaching hurricane force. Comparable to California's Santa Ana.

Skirt:– The only articles of clothing Miranda owns. And dresses, of course. Robes. No pants, no shorts, no capris. She once helped me dig postholes for the fenceline while wearing patent-leather heels, pearls and cashmere. She held the digging bar while I wrestled stones from the earth.

Songe:– French for dream. *En français dans le texte.*

Soprano:– The best of all possible human voices. Flits about in the range of two octaves above middle C. Some can comfortably climb to high F. But I always lose track of such things when listening to Miranda.

Sorceress:– English translation of my first intimate term for Miranda: Sorcière. The word carries much more favorable connotations in French than in English.

Sovereignty:– Chaucerian term, beloved of the Wife of Bath. Experience is her teacher, and she's learned women most desire Sovereignty.

Spline:– A thin decorative and structural strip of wood used in joinery.

Starling:– A small non-native bird which plagues North America in great numbers. It was imported by devotees of Shakespeare, who mentions it, once. It does tremendous damage to crops.

Straight-toned:– An abhorrent method of singing, popularized by barbershop quartets, now invading choirs and the like. Vibrato has far more passion, which may explain why unimaginative and passionless choir directors prefer straight tone.

Stucco:– An exterior housing decorative finish popular in dry climates. In the East, sometimes used for interior finishes in public buildings.

Sumeria:– Site of the oldest recorded poetry (4th millennium BCE). Their goddess of love was named Inanna, and served as a model for others.

Sycamore:– A secondary wood used in furniture making for the hidden sides of drawers and other structural elements which won't be seen. Also, the largest trees on the floodplain behind the house. Grapevines hang from the lowest branches, ideal for boys desiring to imitate Tarzan.

Synchronicity:– I'm not normally fond of Jung, but I like this idea: that two things or events, not causally related, can occur together in meaningful ways. Each experience of Miranda's love is an ideal example of synchronicity. Under Littlewood's Law, such miracles only happen about once a month.

Talavera:– A type of tile distinguished by the fine quality of the native clay. Originally from the Talavera region of Spain (Toledo province), now specifically from the Puebla State of Mexico. Technically known as *Talavera Poblana*. The tiles themselves are often a deep blue. Its milky white glaze must always be crazed.

Tapa:– Decorative cloth woven from pounded bark strips of the Paper Mulberry. Often 'painted' with extracts from the Koka tree.

Tara:– Asian goddess of compassion and enlightened activity, worshiped by both men and women.

Tessalate:– The use of small square stones to form a mosaic pattern in tile, icons, or on the floors of a cathedral.

Tessitura:– The texture, timbre, or pitch range of a singer's natural voice. Also, sudden or gradual rises and falls in pitch during a song.

Thinset:– Adhesive cement-like mortar used in the process of setting tile. The less you use, the better the tile will look.

Throat-singing:– Overtone singing consisting of diverse and complex resonances. Tibetan Buddhist chanting is one example.

Thunbergia:– Here, a black-eyed Susan vine, a small rampant annual which grows well when held aloft by the strands of ornamental grasses.

Torc:– A form of ancient Celtic jewelry. If gold or silver, they go well with Miranda's jewel tones.

Torquing:– I've completely given up on screwdrivers, precisely because of torquing forces. I use a small electric drill instead.

Transept:– The transverse section of a cruciform cathedral, sometimes referred to as the wings of the church.

Transfiguration:– A change, especially in surface appearance, but sometimes, as here, also in essence.

Transversal:– A line stretching across another line at an angle. Here, the lines of waves broke at an angle against the reef.

Trilliums:– Small tri-petaled flowers (wakerobins, birthroot), which grow in the floodplain woodlands behind our home.

Tripoli:– A fine polishing compound used in lapidary and woodturning.

Triptych:– A three sided painting in which similar or related subjects are seen. Sometimes three views of a single subject. Here, Miranda's beauty is seen from three related angles.

Trope:– Any change of a word from a literal sense to the figurative. All metaphors are tropes. See Stevens: "This trivial trope reveals a way of truth."

Tung:– Oil refined from a Chinese Tung tree, often employed as a finish by expert woodworkers. Pure tung oil should be avoided, as I learned to my pain, as each coat can take weeks to cure. At least the final result buffed up well.

Undertone:– In music, an undercurrent of sound, often barely audible. In painting, a color onto which other colors are overlaid. In poetry, the expectation given by the establishment of rhythm, against which variants are measured.

Unicursal:– Possessed of, or consisting of, a single curve. Most often used in connection with meditative spiral labyrinths.

Unmixed:– In Roman times, especially during the ages of Ovid and Martial, wine was always mixed with water in civilized settings. Some of the best wines of the age came from Latium, specifically Falaria.

Urchin:– Spiky sea creature. Miranda stepped on one in St. Thomas. I had to carry her all the way across the reef, and bind the wound on shore.

Utpalas:– The blossom of a blue lotus (Nymphaea Caerulea). Also, a mythological being, a commentary on an Indian poem, or the feminine name of a river. Take your pick.

Venetian plaster:– A wall treatment involving plaster mixed with marble dust, applied in layers and burnished when dry. Miranda suggested it for the living room. It looked wonderful, but took forever. The burnishing is endless.

Vibrato:– Regular, pulsing, natural changes of pitch in a singer's voice. While all human voices possess the capacity to produce vibrato, Miranda's is particularly fine.

Victimae Paschali Laudes:– One of the stranger hymns in the chant repertoire. Often sung at Easter. Literally: Now let us praise the Pascal Victim. It dates to Wipo of Burgundy, an 11th Century chaplain.

***Vin de Diable*:**– Another name for Champagne: The Devil's Vintage. Some say the term developed because the bottles would sometimes explode, even at table, as if possessed. Others say it was so named because consumption led to indiscretions by young women, who were otherwise chaste. Additional explanations are speculative, at best.

Vitrified:– Certain kinds of stone or tile, when exposed to heat, pressure, or sunlight over very long periods, actually take on some of the properties of glass.

Voyage de Noces:– A more elegant French term for Honeymoon.

Warring States:– A period of Chinese history, from around 500 BCE to 221 BCE. The upheavals spawned many mythic and romantic tales. Often compared to the Arthurian period of English history.

Whistler:– American painter (1834-1903), whose *Peacock Room* is crucial to Miranda's story.

Willow:– The corkscrew willow is a fast-growing weeping tree. Particularly vibrant, they arrived in this country when packing materials made of willow stems were discarded onto moist ground, and the stems rooted. They surround our back fence.

Windandsea:– My favorite beach in California. There's no parking, and a significant undertow. Don't attempt to go swimming there, the riptides can carry you all the way to Mexico.

Wisteria:– My favorite flowering vine. They take five years to grow from new planting to blossom. For this reason, until I met Miranda, I'd never actually flowered one. Luckily, her favorite color is purple.

Wonderboard:– Rigid fiberglass and cement underlayment intended for use in setting tile.

Workbench:– One of the great ironies of woodworking is that you need a bench in order to make a bench. And if the old bench isn't perfectly flat, the new bench will be skewed in exactly the same way.

Yungas:– A region of South America stretching from Peru to Bolivia. Coca is a primary crop. Known to North Americans for the "*Camino de la muerte*."

Index

Poem titles are in bold and the first lines are in regular text with page numbers on the right.

A dove along the roofline, still unseen,	*14*
A single candle serves. A small lamplight,	*34*
A Tail Full of Suns	**97**
A thousand voices clamour in my head,	*5*
Adornments	**30**
Amber	**92**
An egg has feathers, and a chestnut horse,	*102*
An ordinary morning: as she wakes,	*38*
Anacostia	**29**
And she, this morning, in my arms became,	*28*
Arrival	**17**
Arts and Mysteries	**61**
At first, I thought them legends: Warring States,	*73*
Balloon or bird above the waving trees,	*98*
Barely recalling patterns roseate,	*17*
Bent to cramped knees, a chisel in your hand,	*69*
Beyond the house, beyond the fence I built,	*63*
Carmina Burana	**7**
Catalog	**6**
Censer	**65**
Chanticleer	**8**
Château Miranda	**68**
Cleaning my shop, I find a strip of lath,	*65*
Clear sky past dawn, rose granite peaks, moraine,	*101*
Cloud Ladders	**102**
Coloratura	**22**
Columbina	**77**
Compline	**105**
Constructing Beauty	**68**
Convocation	**23**
Cymatics	**103**
Dalliance	**20**
Darkness, sometime near three, when we both wake,	*60*
Departure	**106**
Disorder	**50**
Does sound have form? And can we illustrate,	*103*
Double Vision	**98**

Drawn lights. The blinds descending. No disguise,	19
Epilogue	**109**
Evanescence	**90**
Exploration	**18**
First have a plan in mind. A crowbar will,	58
Fisher	**101**
Flow	**44**
Folklife Festival	**96**
Forget, a moment, everything you know:, Back Cover	
Glass Harmonica	**86**
Gold	**80**
Good mortises are difficult. The grain,	59
Grace	**89**
Green gold and blue, the Whistler, stylized,	97
Green Tara	**15**
Her breasts exposed, light handed, out of time,,	75
Her eyes are open as she walks across,	33
Her form is my enchantment, wrapped in lace,	16
Her veil, lifting, overcomes my gaze,,	26
Hinges	**59**
I built each feature of this empty room,	66
I can remember other concerts played,	94
I cannot step outside myself for you,	22
I did not know her when my train traversed,	9
I have not yet discovered why the earth,	3
I know these mountains: above timberline,	55
I lose myself each eventide and must,	35
I made my love a garden of these songs:,	109
I read on summer evenings. Reclined,,	36
I stop. For now it's finished. All around,	108
I wanted to write paradise. I would,	107
I watch the tiny shorebirds interweave,	44
I whisper in her ear each morning songs,	40
I would unlearn this gift, and make a song,	110
I'll always carry matches with me now.,	88
I've made a life of losing everything.,	52
In ancient times, ten suns circled our land,	72
In ringing midnight, bells are not consumed,	105
In Rockville as she drank her coffee, they,	12
In silent concert hastening along,	64
Incarnant Sounds	**108**
It only happens to the fallen. Trees,	68
It's easy to forget. I don't forget:,	10

It's not enough to twine these copper strands,	*62*
Jewelweed	**56**
Jouissance	***67***
June hurricanes are coming on again:,	*54*
Just outside Mobile Bay, a thunderstorm,	*104*
La Belle	**38**
Labyrinth	**85**
Landscape	**42**
Last Saturday, I took James for a walk.,	*50*
Le Vin du Diable	***48***
Lied du Chêne	***91***
Listening	**5**
Look there: the forest, leafed now with its green,	*53*
Lotus	**28**
Love Sings Us From This Life	**2**
Magic	**11**
Mayday	**32**
Melusine	**75**
Memory	**10**
Mendelssohn	**88**
Meteors	**3**
Mirabai	**16**
Miraculous your subtle nakedness,	*30*
Miranda	**41**
Mirrors	**74**
Mistrust my words, take all in wariness,	*21*
Misunderstanding	**51**
Möbius, Back Cover	
Mousetrap	**60**
My love becomes another when I take,	*27*
My mind is always autumn when I think,	*39*
My only gift is love: I sing light songs,	*2*
Mysteries	**33**
Near equinox red seeds hand scattered sprout,	*80*
Night Pearls	**73**
No man should have to risk his life for leaves.,	*93*
No mask: her blush the object of this scene,,	*77*
Old Polynesians fabricated guards,	*90*
On Learning How to Read	**36**
On scales held by Aphrodite, weighed,	*74*
Open your eyes. The beast prepares to feed,	*31*
Our August forest blossoms, but these trees,	*67*
Our cashier bore a tattoo on his arm.,	*100*

Our forest isn't much for rattlesnakes,,	56
Our graduation ceremonials,	48
Our spring comes late this year: those peregrines,	51
Our trees are blossoming. They almost burn,	77
Outside, the irises are withered blades.,	42
Passionate Virtuosity	62
Perhaps she was the daughter of the moon,	78
Photograph	99
Prayer	55
Prey	31
Prosody	64
Rasa	39
Raven	72
Redemption	76
Reflections	46
Renewal	27
Restoration	34
Resurrection Fern	104
Return	47
Revery	26
Revision	35
Ritual	66
Rough congealations of the frozen sea,,	92
Rutter's Requiem	94
She casts a circle somewhere in this room,	15
She did not ask, though others had, for some,	11
She did not need a skirt sewn through with coins,	4
She dreams of houses she had never known,	37
She's looking at me as she looks away,	99
Shorelines	9
Silk Road	81
Since spring has come, I walk the riverwood,	29
Since that first fall along the shoreline I've,	41
Songe	37
Sorceress	12
Sovereignty	63
Spinning Wheel	79
Spinning Yarns	40
St. Thomas	45
Stone Cutters	84
Storm	54
Strange mysteries of incense and of smoke,	23
Sumeria	78
Synchronicity	21

Talavera	58
Tatu	100
The Dark Wood	107
The garden outside sunlit from the east,,	13
The Mall in Washington: extended green,	96
The porch, unpainted, falls to disrepair,	89
The red cloth in a basin, lavender,	20
The small oaks of the maquis countryside,	91
The stage is blank now. Ribbons swirling, smoke,	81
The Structure of Desire	4
Theological College	87
These bowls, spindled, confuse. So painted red,	86
These tessalate lunations, vitrified,	85
This forest should be all our thought today,	32
This morning, a young boy, in sleepy haste,	46
This unfamiliar azure, with its waves,	24
Tide pools. Sunlight. Shorebirds overhead.,	45
Transformation	14
Triptych	19
Tulip magnolias through leaded glass:,	87
Twelve voices, singing. A constructed hymn.,	8
Two deer graze underneath those windmill trees,	47
Venetian plaster, tablecloths, a long,	6
Victimae Paschali Laudes	49
Visionary	53
Visitation	13
Voyage de Noces	24
We do it now with saws. Back then, a sledge,	84
We rush through all: Champagne Rosé, Bordeaux,	7
We walk in, barely late. The choir ends.,	49
We walk the Vermont landscape looking for,	61
What is this wind encircling us that binds,	18
Wind	110
Within my arms, her listening consumes,	79
Within this circle her embellished hand,	106
Wrenhouse	52
Yungas Valley	93

PUBLICATION CREDITS

Grateful acknowledgement is made to the editors of the following publications in which some of the poems from *The Structure of Desire* first appeared:

Aesthetica (UK): "Talavera"
Anthropology and Humanism Journal: "Yungas Valley"
Booth: A Journal: "Sovereignty"
Broad River Review: "Grace"
Cha: An Asian Literary Journal (China): "Silk Road"
Common Ground Review: "Sorceress"
Crucible: "Prosody"
Ellen LaForge Poetry Prize Annual: "Cymatics," "Landscape," "Rasa," "Storm," "Wrenhouse"
Heartland Review: "Flow"
Innisfree Poetry Journal: "Renewal"
Interrobang Magazine: "Victimae Paschali Laudes"
Istanbul Literary Review (Turkey): "Green Tara," "Miranda"
Kestrel: A Journal of Literature and Art: "Spinning Wheel"
Kritya Journal of Poetry (India): "Wind"
Little Red Tree International Poetry Prize Anthology: "Adornments," "On Learning How To Read," "The Structure of Desire."
Moments of the Soul: Spirit First Anthology: "Compline."
Old Red Kimono: "Restoration"
Open Road Review (India): "Listening"
Permafrost, A Literary Journal: "Resurrection Fern"
Poetry Salzburg Review (Austria): "Constructing Beauty," "Gold"
Potomac Review: "Photograph"
Sea Stories: "St. Thomas"
Snakeskin (UK): "Jewelweed"
Soundzine: "Carmina Burana"
String Poet: "Visionary," "Magic"
Swale Life (UK): "Mousetrap"
The Linnet's Wing (Ireland): "La Belle," "Rutter's Requiem"
Thema: Music and Math: "Chanticleer"
THIS Literary Magazine: "Revision," "Sumeria"
Think Journal: "Misunderstanding"
Umbrella Journal: "Disorder," "Möbius"
Unsplendid: "Catalog"
Valparaiso Fiction Review: Foreword as "Requiem"

About the Author

W.F. Lantry

W.F. Lantry, native of San Diego, is a widely published prize winning poet who has been featured in poetry journals and readings nationally and internationally. He currently lives in Washington, DC.

Lantry worked with Carolyn Forché in California, where he founded and edited *Eye Prayers*, a small press journal of poetry. He taught for eight years at *L'Université de Nice* in France earning his *License* and *Maîtrise* in English Literature, Linguistics and Translation. During this time, he won the Paris/Atlantic Young Writers Award. Boston University awarded him a Fellowship to study with Derek Walcott and George Starbuck, who together directed his thesis. There he received an M.A. in English and Creative Writing. He holds a PhD in Literature and Creative Writing from the University of Houston where he worked with Donald Barthelme, Ed Hirsch, Mary Robison, James Robison and Adam Zagajewski. He was the first in the program to be awarded a double PhD, one in Fiction, one in Poetry. He has taught at

12 different Universities on two continents in a variety of fields, most often Literature and Rhetoric, but also in History, Library Science, World Civilizations, and Information Technology. He served as Director of Academic Technology at a national research university in Washington, DC for 15 years.

His recent honors include:

2012
Potomac Review Poetry Prize
Old Red Kimono LaNelle Daniel Prize
The Linnet's Wing (Ireland) Audio Poetry Prize

2011
Crucible Editors' Poetry Prize
Atlanta Review International Publication Prize

2010
CutBank Patricia Goedicke Prize in Poetry
Lindberg Foundation International Poetry for Peace Prize (Israel)
National Hackney Literary Award in Poetry
Comment Magazine Poetry Competition (first place)

He has twice been named finalist in the *Premio Mundial Fernando Rielo de Poesía Mística* (Spain). In 2010, he was named runner up for the UMB William Joiner Center Ellen LaForge Poetry Prize and the Hong Kong University Poetry Book Prize (China), he was commended for his entry in the International Hippocrates Prize for Poetry and Medicine (UK), and in Canada received Honorable Mention for the *Prairie Fire* Banff Centre Bliss Carman Poetry Award. In 2012, he was nominated for five Pushcart Prizes in two genres on three continents. He has given readings of his poetry in California, Texas, Connecticut, Tennessee, Massachusetts, Pennsylvania and Washington, DC.

While in Nice, he participated in *Interspace*, a project seeking to unify Poetry, Philosophy, Music and Visual Art. As part of the *Interspace* project, he gave readings at the *Musée Chéret* and *Galerie Ponchettes* in Nice, Centre Pompidou in Paris, *La Sapienza, Università di Roma* in Italy and collaborated on a multi media event presented at the *Roccabella* in Monte Carlo under the patronage of and hosted by Prince Albert.

In the past year he was featured in the DC area at the *HearArts* Spoken Word & Music Program in Rockville, the Takoma Park Poetry Reading Series and the Poetry Lab Series at The Soundry in Northern Virginia. Other recent engagements include the *Kestrel* Celebration at Fairmont State University, and in New York at The Poets House, the Dada Poetry Salon Series at Cornelia St. Café, the *Fiele-Festa* launch at KGB, and the *String Poet* Studio Series at the Long Island Violin Shop.

His publication credits (listed separately) encompass print and online journals and anthologies, with his work translated into French, Arabic, Italian and Uzbek. He was the founding featured author of *Eclectica*, and new work has appeared in numerous publications in many countries including: Canada, Mexico, Scotland, France, Germany, Austria, Czech Republic, Syria, Bosnia & Herzegovina, Turkey, Israel, India, Indonesia, India, China and the UK.

Recently *THIS Literary Magazine* selected him as Spotlight Poet, and *The Tower Journal* featured his work. His chapbook, *The Language of Birds,* is a lyric retelling of Attar's *Conference of the Birds*. *The Structure of Desire* (Little Red Tree Press) is his first full-length collection.

LITTLE RED TREE PUBLISHING

Little Red Tree Publishing, established in 2006 by Michael Linnard and Tamara Martin is based in New London, CT. Taking as their motto "delight, entertain and educate," they strive to combine their love of quality books with an interest in fiction, non-fiction, poetry, music, art, design, history and photography. From the start they defined themselves, consistent with the finest traditions of small independent publishing, as preserving and expanding the dwindling opportunities for previously unknown poets and established poets to publish a full collection of poetry. They passionately believe that well crafted books and accessible poetry should be celebrated and presented as such with conviction and confidence. Therefore, all books are coffee table size, 7" by 10" or above – an emphatic statement of intent and a celebration of the poetry. Little Red Tree is named after a Japanese Maple (Acer Palmatum), planted in 2005, and both still thrive. Below is a selection from the 32 books published since 2006.

All the dead goats
by Nikoletta Nousiopoulos

Crossing Over
by William Meredith

San Francisco Poems
by A.D. Winans

Clair-Obscur of the Soul
by Jean-Yves Solinga

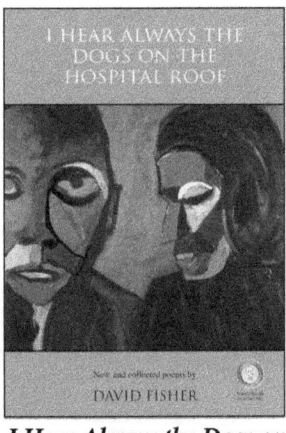

I Hear Always the Dogs on the Hospital Roof
by David Fisher

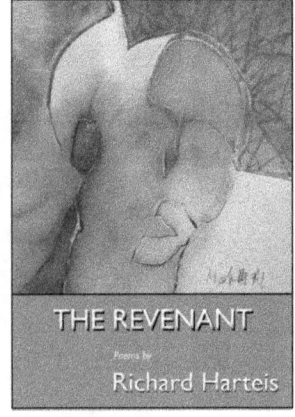

The Revenant
by Richard Harteis

www.ingramcontent.com/pod-product-compliance
Lightning Source LLC
Chambersburg PA
CBHW080508110426
42742CB00017B/3031